SPACE
ACTIVITY
LAB

Senior editor Michelle Crane
Senior designer Stefan Podhorodecki
US senior editor Kayla Dugger
US executive editor Lori Hand

Managing editor Francesca Baines
Managing art editor Philip Letsu
Senior production editor Gillian Reid
Production controller Jack Matts
Jacket designer Stephanie Cheng Hui Tan
Design development manager Sophia MTT
Senior jackets coordinator Priyanka Sharma-Saddi
Jacket DTP designer Rakesh Kumar
Picture researcher Myriam Megharbi

Publisher Andrew Macintyre
Art director Karen Self
Associate publishing director Liz Wheeler
Publishing director Jonathan Metcalf

Consultant Giles Sparrow
Photographer Nigel Wright
Illustrator Simon Tegg

PRODUCED FOR DK BY:
XAB Design
Designers Nigel Wright, Jan Browne
Art direction Nigel Wright
Project creation Nigel Wright
Project editor Stephanie Farrow

First American Edition, 2023
Published in the United States by DK Publishing
1745 Broadway, 20th Floor, New York, NY 10019

Copyright © 2023 Dorling Kindersley Limited
DK, a Division of Penguin Random House LLC
23 24 25 26 27 10 9 8 7 6 5 4 3 2 1
001–335832–Aug/2023

A catalog record for this book
is available from the Library of Congress.
ISBN: 978-0-7440-8223-4

DK books are available at special discounts when purchased
in bulk for sales promotions, premiums, fund-raising,
or educational use. For details, contact:
DK Publishing Special Markets,
1745 Broadway, 20th Floor, New York, NY 10019
SpecialSales@dk.com

Printed and bound in China

For the curious
www.dk.com

Smithsonian

The Smithsonian

Established in 1846, the Smithsonian is the world's largest
museum and research complex, dedicated to public education,
national service, and scholarship in the arts, sciences, and
history. It includes 19 museums and galleries and the
National Zoological Park. The total number of artifacts,
works of art, and specimens in the Smithsonian's
collection is estimated at 154 million.

SMITHSONIAN

SPACE
ACTIVITY
LAB

EXCITING SPACE PROJECTS FOR
BUDDING ASTRONOMERS

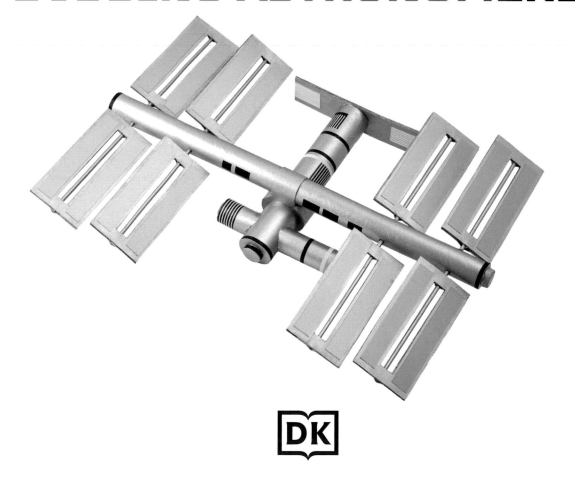

DK

CONTENTS

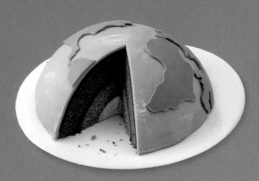

STEM FACTS
This symbol highlights extra information that explains the learning behind a project.

SPACE FACTS
This symbol flags up extra information about space and space exploration.

WARNING
This symbol identifies a task that might be dangerous. Be sure to have adult supervision.

A WORD ABOUT GLUES
Several of the projects in this book require the use of glue. We've suggested that you use ordinary white glue or glue sticks, but in some cases it will be easier to use a glue gun if you have one, as this glue dries much faster. A glue gun should only ever be used by an adult, and they must be sure to follow the manufacturer's guidelines.

A WORD ABOUT MESS!
Some of these projects can be messy (especially the one that involves making papier mâché), so check with an adult on where you can set up your workstation.

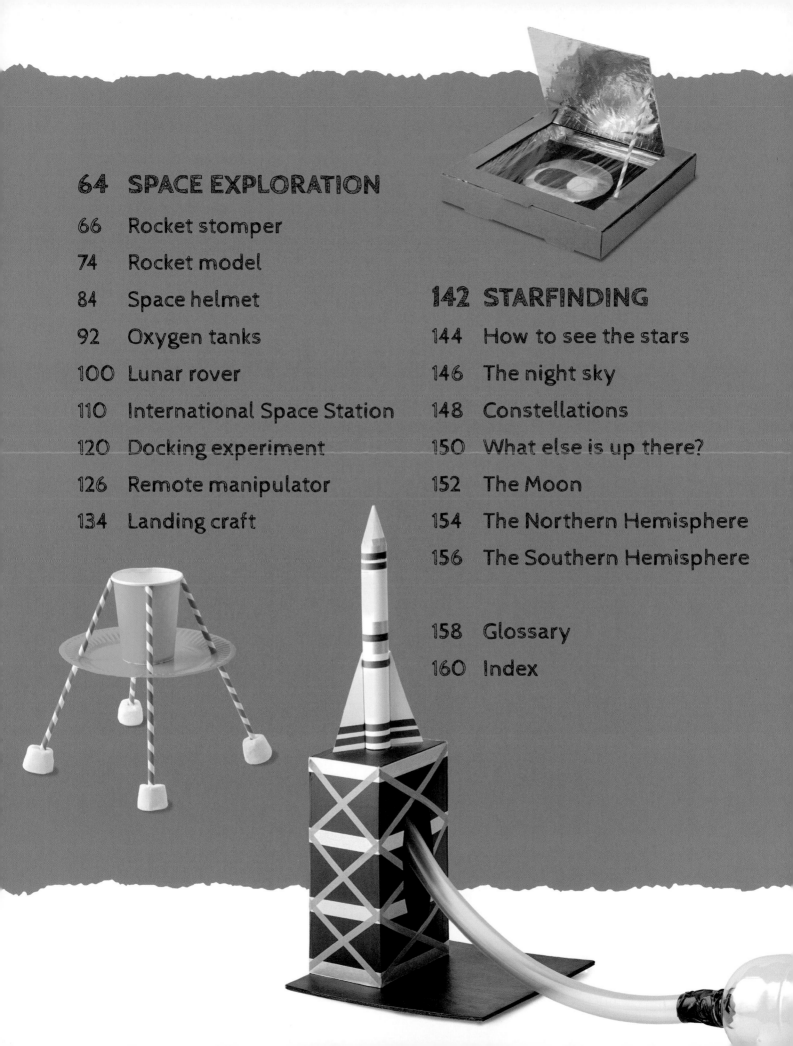

THE SOLAR SYSTEM

Our planet is one of eight in our Solar System, all orbiting the brilliant star we call the Sun. This chapter will help you explore how we see planets, galaxies, stars, and constellations from Earth. Learn about the power of the Sun; how to predict the phases of the Moon; and how orbits, gravity, and eclipses work. You'll learn about the layers of our own planet, Earth, too, and about the rocks, or meteorites, that land on it from space.

SUN CLOCK

As our planet spins each day, the shadows cast by the Sun move.
You can use those shadows to tell the time, working out your position
in relation to the Sun, then marking off the hours on your own sundial
as the Sun moves across the sky.

MEASURING SOLAR TIME

The changing position of the
Sun in the sky can be used to
measure what's called "local
solar time." A sundial tracks
this position using a shadow
cast by the Sun.

The upright part
of the sundial, which
casts the shadow, is
called a gnomon.

The gnomon slope
ensures that shadows
always fall in the
same direction at
the same local time.

The shadow moves
as the Sun travels
across the sky.

You'll need a compass
to align your gnomon
with the North or
South Pole.

MAKE YOUR OWN
SUNDIAL

It won't take you long to make this simple cardstock sundial, but you'll need a sunny day to mark off the hours on it. Watch the shadow move as time ticks by and make your own marks from sunrise to sunset.

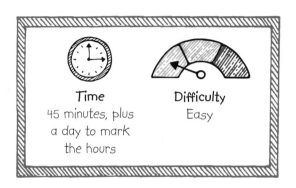

Time
45 minutes, plus a day to mark the hours

Difficulty
Easy

WHAT YOU NEED

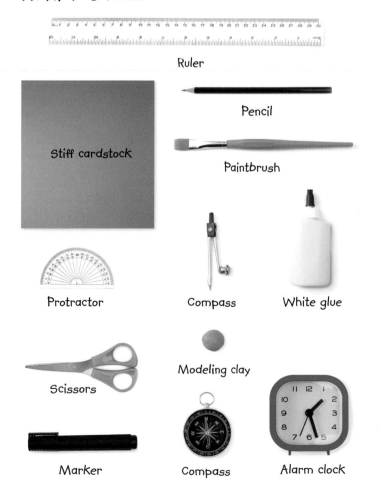

Ruler

Pencil

Stiff cardstock

Paintbrush

Protractor

Compass

White glue

Modeling clay

Scissors

Marker

Compass

Alarm clock

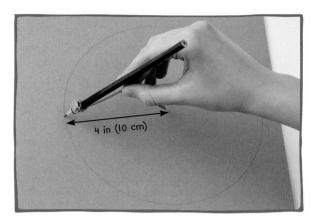

1 To make the base, set your compass to a radius of 4 in (10 cm) and draw a circle onto cardstock. Cut it out, then cut two more the same size.

4 in (10 cm)

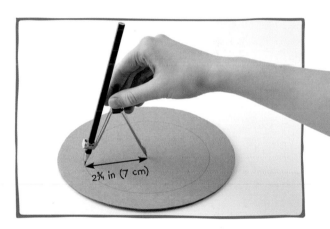

2¾ in (7 cm)

2 Inside one of the circles, with your compass at the same central point, draw an inner circle with a radius of 2¾ in (7 cm).

3 To cut out the inner circle, make a hole with a pencil. (Put modeling clay behind for protection.) Put scissors into the hole and cut around the line.

For the gnomon slot, draw parallel lines on either side of the center line.

4 Draw a center line across a circle. On the line, mark off 1¾ in (4.5 cm) and 5⁵⁄₁₆ in (13.5 cm). Add parallel lines ⅛ in (2 mm) on either side, between the marks.

5 Using modeling clay and a pencil again, carefully make a hole in the cardstock between the outer parallel lines, then cut out the slot.

The angle you need here depends on your latitude (see box below).

6 Draw a line 3⁹⁄₁₆ in (9 cm) from an edge of a piece of cardstock. Add a second line, at a right angle, ¾ in (2 cm) from the adjacent edge to make a tab.

7 Use a protractor to draw a diagonal line at the angle of your latitude from the end of the tab line across to the first line.

WHERE ARE YOU?

To cast the right shadow, a sundial's gnomon must tilt toward the North or South Pole (whichever is closest to you) at the same angle as its latitude. This is a measure of location on Earth, north or south of the equator. Ask an adult to help you find your latitude on a map, and use that angle for the diagonal line of your gnomon.

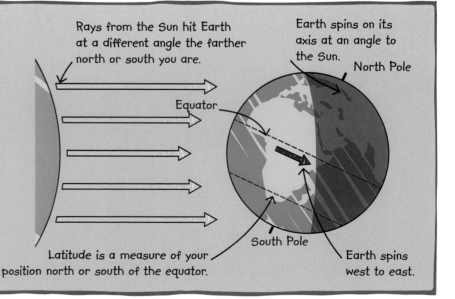

Rays from the Sun hit Earth at a different angle the farther north or south you are.

Earth spins on its axis at an angle to the Sun.

North Pole

Equator

South Pole

Earth spins west to east.

Latitude is a measure of your position north or south of the equator.

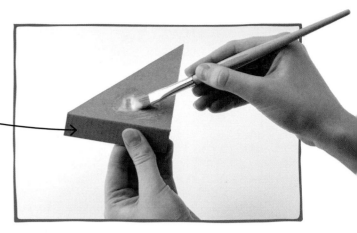

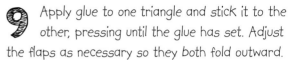

Keep the two tabs clear of glue when you stick the triangles together.

8 Cut out the triangle, then copy it to cut a second triangle. Fold the two tabs along the ¾-in (2-cm) lines. (Use a ruler for a sharp crease.)

9 Apply glue to one triangle and stick it to the other, pressing until the glue has set. Adjust the flaps as necessary so they both fold outward.

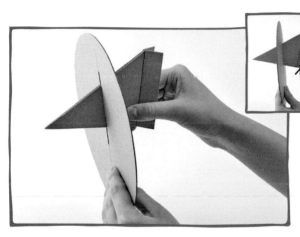

Put glue on the inside of each tab.

10 Carefully push the gnomon through the slot in the circle. Apply glue to the inside of the tabs, nearest the circle.

11 Push the gnomon right through as far as the tabs, then hold the two tabs flush against the circle until set.

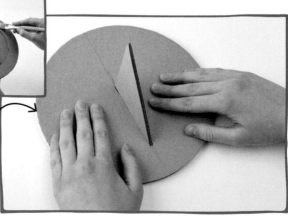

The circle underneath encloses the tabs to ensure that the base sits flat.

The ring sits around the tabs, flush with the circle.

12 Next, apply glue to one side of the ring you made in Step 3. Stick it to the same side of the circle as the tabs, being careful of the gnomon.

13 Apply glue to the ring and position it on top of the remaining cardstock circle to complete your base. Press firmly until set.

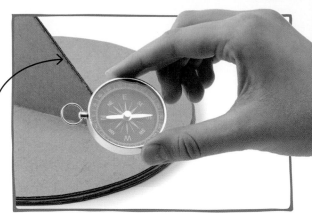

Align the sundial by looking upward along the slope of the gnomon from the base.

14 On a sunny day, at sunrise, take the sundial outside and put it on a flat surface that will stay in full sun all day. Set an alarm clock to ring on the hour, every hour.

15 Use a compass to line up the gnomon with north if you are in the Northern Hemisphere or south if you are in the Southern Hemisphere (see box, page 10).

Mark off the hours on the base of your sundial.

16 At the first hour, mark where the shadow falls on your sundial. Repeat every time the alarm rings to mark each hour. By sunset, you will have all the daylight hours marked on your base.

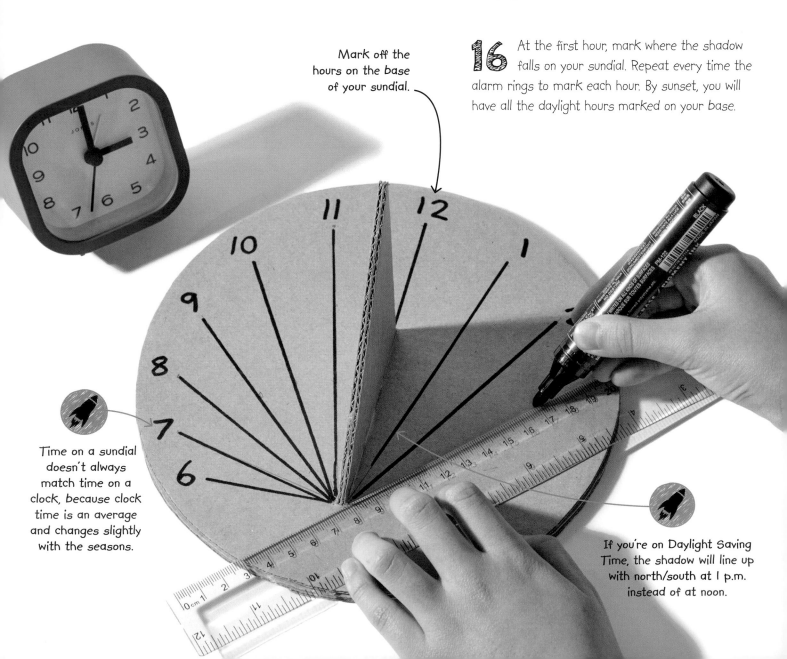

Time on a sundial doesn't always match time on a clock, because clock time is an average and changes slightly with the seasons.

If you're on Daylight Saving Time, the shadow will line up with north/south at 1 p.m. instead of at noon.

HOW IT WORKS

As Earth spins west to east in the course of a day, the Sun moves through the sky. The shadows it casts are always on the opposite side from the Sun, and the length and direction of the shadows also changes.

When the Sun is directly overhead, it casts a short shadow, but as it travels across the sky and the angle at which its rays reach you changes, your shadow also lengthens. Whether you are in the Northern or Southern Hemisphere will determine if you need to point your gnomon to the North Pole or the South Pole, and where you are on the planet will also affect that angle, so the slope of the gnomon needs to match that (see box, page 10).

NORTH OF THE EQUATOR

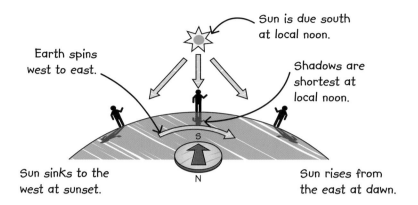

Earth spins west to east.

Sun is due south at local noon.

Shadows are shortest at local noon.

Sun sinks to the west at sunset.

Sun rises from the east at dawn.

SOUTH OF THE EQUATOR

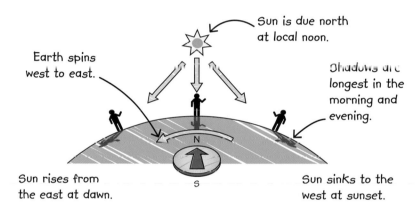

Earth spins west to east.

Sun is due north at local noon.

Shadows are longest in the morning and evening.

Sun rises from the east at dawn.

Sun sinks to the west at sunset.

SPACE SCIENCE
EARLY TIMEKEEPERS

Before mechanical clocks were invented, about 600 years ago, the Sun had long been used to measure time. The ancient Egyptians were using shadows to tell the time more than 5,500 years ago; they erected stone pillars called obelisks to act as giant gnomons. Sundials were vital for sailors, astronomers, and anyone who needed to know the time of day. They came in all shapes and sizes, from huge monuments to ones that could fit in your pocket, such as this tiny pocket sundial.

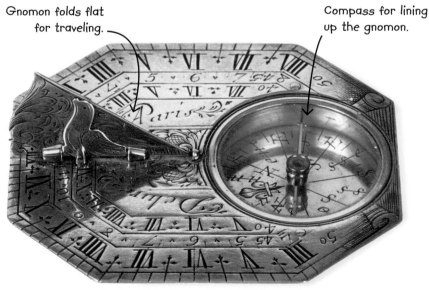

Gnomon folds flat for traveling.

Compass for lining up the gnomon.

A silver 17th-century pocket sundial compass

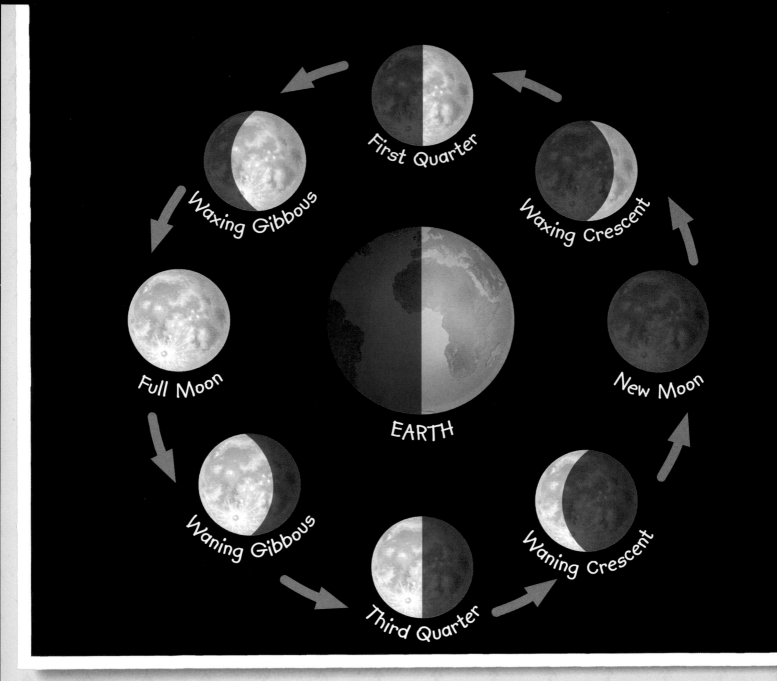

First Quarter

Waxing Crescent

Waxing Gibbous

New Moon

EARTH

Full Moon

Waning Crescent

Waning Gibbous

Third Quarter

TRACKING THE MOON
LUNAR CALENDAR

The Moon's changing shape each night is Known as its "phase." It changes because of the Moon's orbit around Earth, Earth's orbit around the Sun, and the way light bounces off the Moon. Make this lunar tracker to predict what shape the Moon will be next.

THE PHASES OF THE MOON

Although the Moon is the brightest object in the night sky, it doesn't actually give off any light of its own. Instead, it shines by reflecting sunlight. The amount of light illuminating it varies as the angle between the Moon and Sun changes each month. This creates the distinct shapes Known as phases.

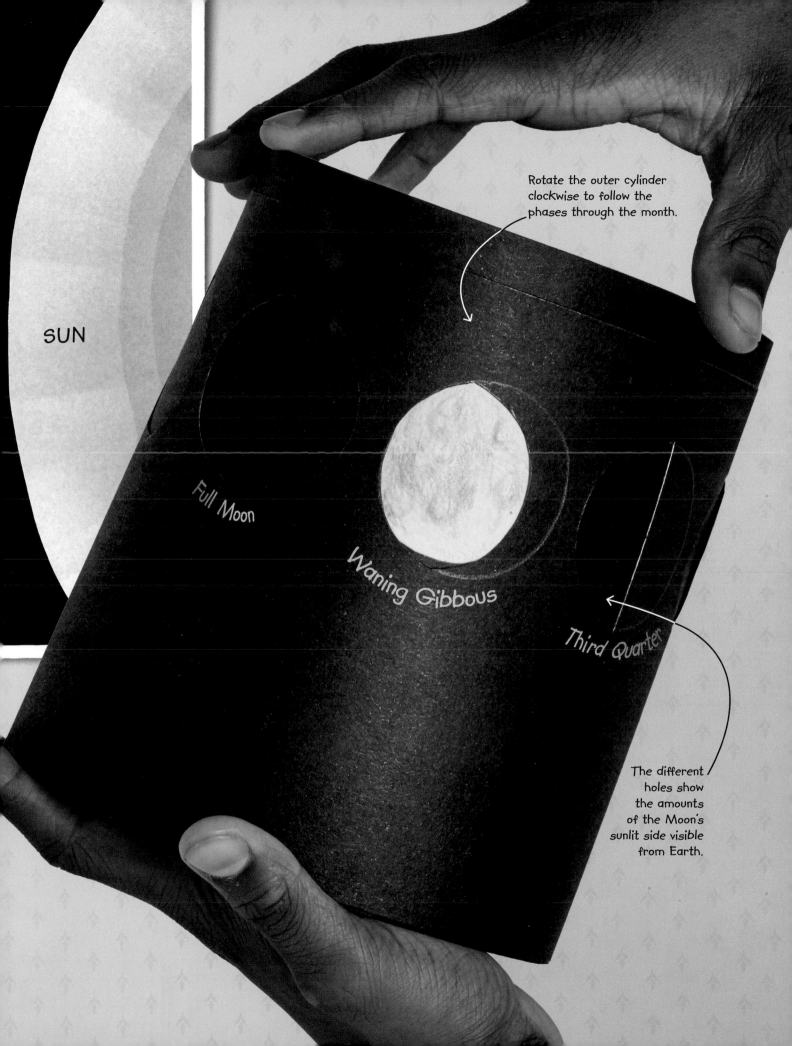

SUN

Rotate the outer cylinder clockwise to follow the phases through the month.

Full Moon

Waning Gibbous

Third Quarter

The different holes show the amounts of the Moon's sunlit side visible from Earth.

MAKE YOUR OWN
LUNAR TRACKER

This clever project will help you learn the phases of the Moon and be able to predict the shape of the Moon in the sky during each month. The two cylinders, one inside the other, work together to show you how much of the Moon you'll *see* in the night *sky* at any time.

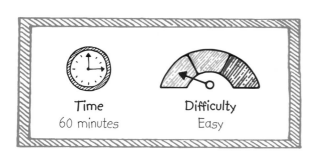

Time
60 minutes

Difficulty
Easy

WHAT YOU NEED

Colored pencils

Scissors

Adhesive tape

Modeling clay

Eraser

White glue

Pencil

Compass

White (or silver) marker

Ruler

Black cardstock

White paper

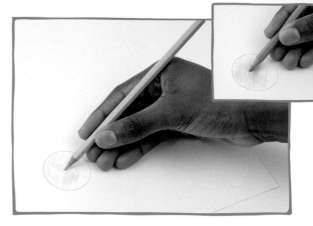

1 On white paper, draw a circle with a radius of ¾ in (2 cm). Color it yellow to look like a shining Moon, add gray shadows, then cut it out.

2 On black cardstock, mark out a rectangular strip measuring 16½ in x 5¹⁵⁄₁₆ in (42 cm x 15 cm). Cut out the strip.

3 Glue the Moon onto the strip about halfway along it and with its edge 1³⁄₁₆ in (3 cm) from one side of the cardstock.

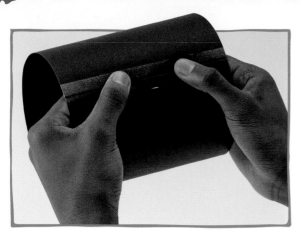

4 With the Moon on the outside, roll the cardstock so that the two short sides overlap slightly. Use adhesive tape to stick the two edges together.

5 You now have a cylinder with the Moon facing outward.

At Full Moon, the Sun lights up the whole of the Moon's Earth-facing side.

6 Cut another strip of *black cardstock* 16½ in × 5½ in (42 cm × 14 cm). Draw eight equally spaced lines about halfway across it. On each line, mark off 1⁹⁄₁₆ in (4 cm) from one edge.

Put the compass point on each mark so your circles are all level.

Divide the length of the strip by eight to work out where the lines sit.

7 Draw a circle with a ¾ in (2 cm) radius around each of the eight marks, then erase the straight lines and marks. With a white marker, label the first circle at the left end "New Moon."

The shading will remind you which area to cut out.

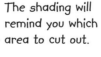

The Moon is "waxing" when the sunlit area is gradually increasing in size.

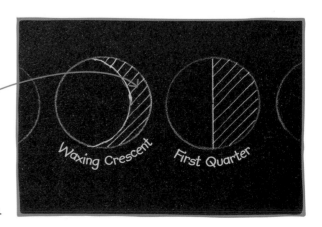

8 In the next circle, draw a crescent, as shown. Draw diagonal lines across the smaller side to shade in the area that will become a hole. Label it "Waxing Crescent."

9 Moving on to the next circle, draw a vertical line down the center, through the compass point, and shade in the area on the right-hand side. Label it "First Quarter."

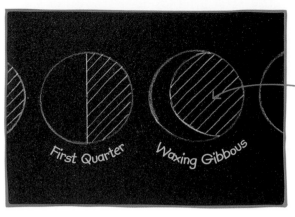

A "gibbous" Moon is one in the midway phase between being half- and fully lit.

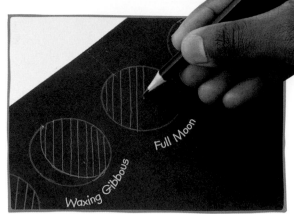

10 Draw a crescent on the left-hand side of the next circle. Label it "Waxing Gibbous" and shade in the larger section.

11 Label the next circle "Full Moon" and shade in the entire shape. For this Moon phase, you're going to cut out the whole circle.

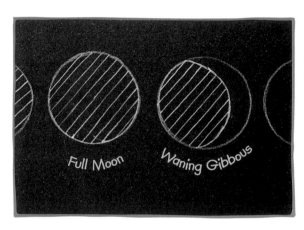

The Moon is "waning" when the area lit by the Sun is gradually decreasing.

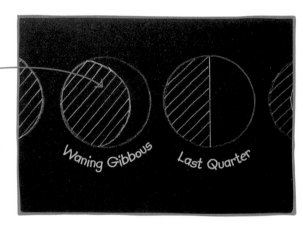

12 In the circle to the right, draw a crescent on the right-hand side and shade the left-hand side. Label it "Waning Gibbous."

13 Draw a vertical line down through the compass point of the next circle and shade the left-hand side. Label it "Last Quarter."

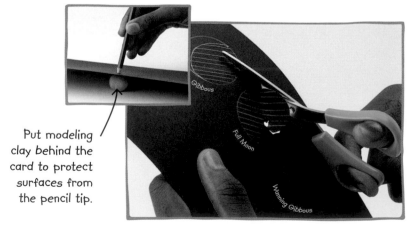

Put modeling clay behind the card to protect surfaces from the pencil tip.

14 On the final circle, draw a crescent on the left-hand side and shade it in. Label it "Waning Crescent."

15 Push a pencil through each of the areas you've shaded to make holes for the scissors, then carefully cut out the shaded areas.

The Moon's orbit around Earth takes 27 days, 8 hours.

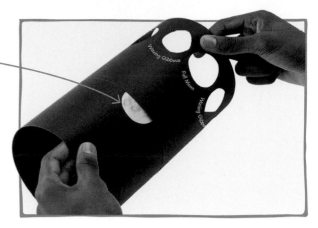

16 Roll the cardstock into a cylinder and tape it up. Butt the two short edges up instead of overlapping them, so it will fit over the first cylinder.

17 Slot the second cylinder over the first one, and line up the Full Moon hole over the colored-in Moon on the inner cylinder.

18 On the next clear evening, check the shape of the Moon in the night sky. Set the outer cylinder to show the Moon on the inner cylinder through the same-shaped hole. Read the label beneath to discover the name of that phase.

FOLLOW THE MOON

To understand how the Moon reflects the light from the Sun, do this experiment in a dark room. You'll need a lamp and a white modeling clay ball stuck on a pencil. The ball is the Moon, the lamp is the Sun, and you are Earth.

1 Hold the ball in front of you, in the full light of the lamp. See how the "Sun" illuminates the full "Moon."

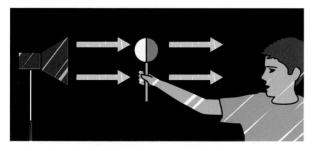

2 Now turn to the left to simulate the Moon orbiting Earth. See the "Moon" appear to change shape as different areas are lit by the "Sun."

What follows? Read the lunar calendar counterclockwise to predict what shape the Moon will make next.

EDIBLE SPACE ROCKS
METEORBITES

In space, the energy released when materials collide can turn into heat and melt them together into space rocks called meteoroids. For this project, you'll use heat to melt chocolate with other sweet treats to make your own "meteorbites" instead. Real space rocks aren't edible, of course, but these are delicious!

WHAT IS A METEORITE?

When specks of dust and small space rocks enter Earth's atmosphere at high speed, they heat up and leave a trail of light known as a meteor or shooting star (see pages 150–151). If one of these makes it through the atmosphere and lands on Earth, it's called a meteorite.

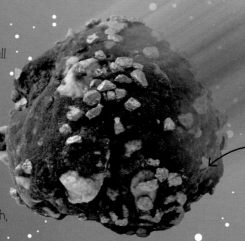

Use lots of different ingredients, as meteorites can be made from all sorts of minerals.

Just like a real meteorite, which burns on its way through the atmosphere, these bites are dark on the outside.

MAKE YOUR OWN
METEORITE BITES

No cooking is required—you just melt the ingredients over a pan of hot water. Don't forget to wash your hands *before* and after handling food.

Time 30 minutes, plus setting time	**Difficulty** Easy	**Warning** Ask an adult for help with boiling water

WHAT YOU NEED

Parchment paper

Tablespoon

Medium-sized saucepan half-full of just-boiled water

Baking sheet

Large heat-resistant bowl

Black food coloring

Wooden spoon

Small shallow bowl

Rolling pin

Ziplock plastic bag

9 oz (250 g) chocolate pieces

4¼ oz (120 g) butter, cubed

2¼ oz (70 g) fudge pieces

¾ oz (20 g) bronze-colored sprinkles

9 oz (250 g) vanilla wafers

2¼ oz (70 g) honeycomb pieces

2½ oz (75 g) mini marshmallows

3 tablespoons light corn syrup

1 Put the wafers in the ziplock bag and seal it. Use a rolling pin to gently break up the wafers into small pieces.

2 Half-fill a saucepan with just-boiled water and put a large bowl over it. Put the butter and chocolate in the bowl, then add the light corn syrup.

3 Gently stir the mixture until all the ingredients have melted together over the boiled water.

Add the food coloring a little at a time.

4 Ask an adult to take the bowl off the saucepan. (It may *be* hot.) Stir in the *black* food coloring until the mixture is a dark color.

The planets and space rocks were also formed by a jumble of materials mixing together.

5 Once you have a dark, gooey mixture, add the broken wafers to the bowl and give everything a stir with the wooden spoon.

Swap in equal amounts of other ingredients if you prefer: nuts, seeds, and dried fruit all work well.

6 Next, add the mini marshmallows and stir them in. Mix everything together.

7 Add the fudge and honeycomb pieces and stir them into the mixture.

8 Finally, add half of the bronze sprinkles (saving the other half for Step 10), then give the mixture one last stir.

Real meteorites can be a mix of many different minerals and elements, such as nickel and iron.

9 Take a golf-ball-sized piece of mixture and mold it into a ball in the palm of your hand. Repeat to turn all the mixture into balls.

10 Put the remaining half of the bronze sprinkles in a shallow bowl and roll each ball around in the sprinkles.

The parchment paper will stop the cakes from sticking to the sheet.

11 Carefully put the balls on a baking sheet that has been lined with a piece of parchment paper.

Cut open a meteorbite to see how the ingredients have melded together.

12 Put the sheet into the fridge and leave the balls to set for an hour or more, then they're ready to eat. Time for a taste of "space"!

SPACE SCIENCE
CHONDRITES

Meteorites come in several types, but chondrites are the oldest and most interesting. Like the meteorbites, they are a jumble of fragments stuck together. Unlike the meteorbite ingredients, however, these fragments are grains of rock and dust that haven't changed since the Solar System was born 4.6 billion years ago.

As tiny fragments collided to form the chondrite, some minerals melted and stuck together, while others remained solid.

COOKING WITH SUN-POWER
SOLAR OVEN

The Sun is Earth's most important source of energy. Tap into that energy to make this solar oven, and experiment to find out how quickly it melts different foods.

SOLAR POWER

The Sun is an incredible nonstop energy machine, with more solar energy reaching Earth's surface in one day than we could use in 27 years! Solar power captures that energy to generate heat and electricity. A solar cooker works by using the Sun's rays to heat up its inner surfaces.

Solar radiation hits the aluminum foil and is reflected onto the food.

The plastic wrap traps heat inside the box, just like the glass in a greenhouse.

Put your food on a matte black background to speed up the heating process.

MAKE YOUR OWN
SOLAR OVEN

Harness the power of the Sun with this solar oven made from a pizza box. (You can order these online.) See how quickly it will "cook" things, but be warned—don't try this on an empty stomach, as it may take some time ...

Time	Difficulty	Warning
30 minutes, plus cooking time	Easy	Ask an adult which foods to use

WHAT YOU NEED

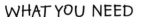

Ruler

Pencil

Scissors

Modeling clay   Compass   White glue

Clean pizza box

Matte black cardstock

Paintbrush

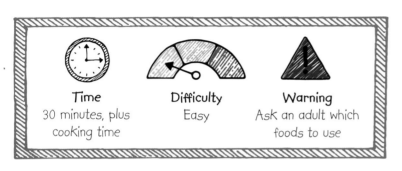

Aluminum foil

Plastic wrap

Drinking straw

Adhesive tape

Foods to cook, such as chocolate and marshmallows

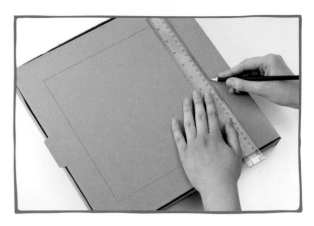

1 To make the oven lid, mark off 1⁹⁄₁₆ in (4 cm) from all four edges of the pizza-box lid. Join the marks to draw a square.

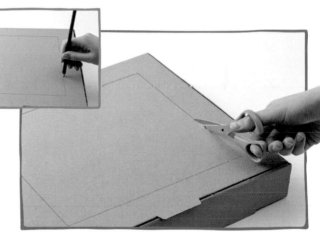

2 Push a pencil through the lid on a line to make a small hole for your scissors. Cut along three lines, but leave the fourth line for the hinge.

3 Bend the square upward to make the hinge. Hold your thumb (or a ruler) on the line to help make the crease, or score it with a pencil first.

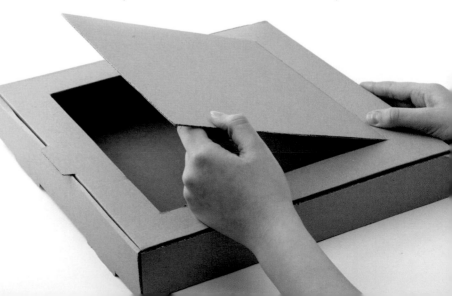

4 Fold the square back until the oven lid opens up completely. Bend the hinge up and down a few times to reinforce the crease.

Aluminum foil will reflect the Sun's rays into your oven.

5 Cut a piece of aluminum foil about the same size as the box and lay it under the oven lid, shiny side down.

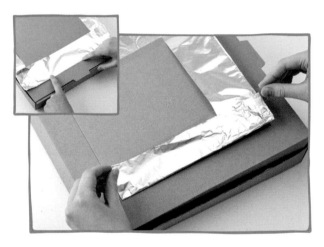

6 Fold the edges of the foil back over the top of the oven lid and tape them in place with strips of adhesive tape.

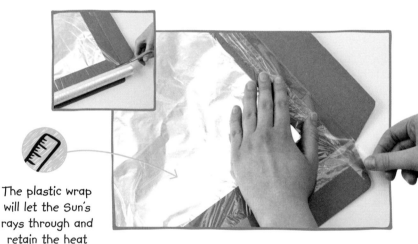

The plastic wrap will let the Sun's rays through and retain the heat generated inside the solar oven.

7 Cut a piece of plastic wrap to the same size as the box. Open out the pizza-box lid and tape the plastic wrap to the inside of it on all four sides.

8 Cut four strips of foil, each as long as one side of the pizza box and about 6 in (15 cm) wide. Fold along one long edge on each strip.

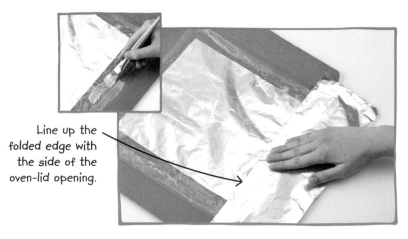

Line up the folded edge with the side of the oven-lid opening.

9 Apply glue onto the plastic wrap and the inside lid. Stick the foil strips on top to line all four sides of the oven lid, then trim off any excess foil.

Black absorbs heat, so it will trap the heat of the Sun in the oven.

10 Line the rest of the inside of the pizza box with foil, first applying glue to the cardstock and then fitting the foil.

11 Cut a square of black cardstock ¾ in (2 cm) smaller than the pizza box. Glue it in position on the inside base of the box, on top of the foil.

Use a compass to draw the circle, or you can draw around a plate.

12 Draw and cut out a circle of cardstock about 6¼ in (16 cm) in diameter. Lay it on the matte side of a piece of foil slightly larger than it.

13 Fold the foil over to wrap the cardstock. Press the foil flat and secure it in place with adhesive tape.

15 Position the solar oven in direct sunlight, and lift up the oven lid.

14 Put the foil circle onto the center of the black square. Now wash your hands, then add your foods and close the pizza-box lid.

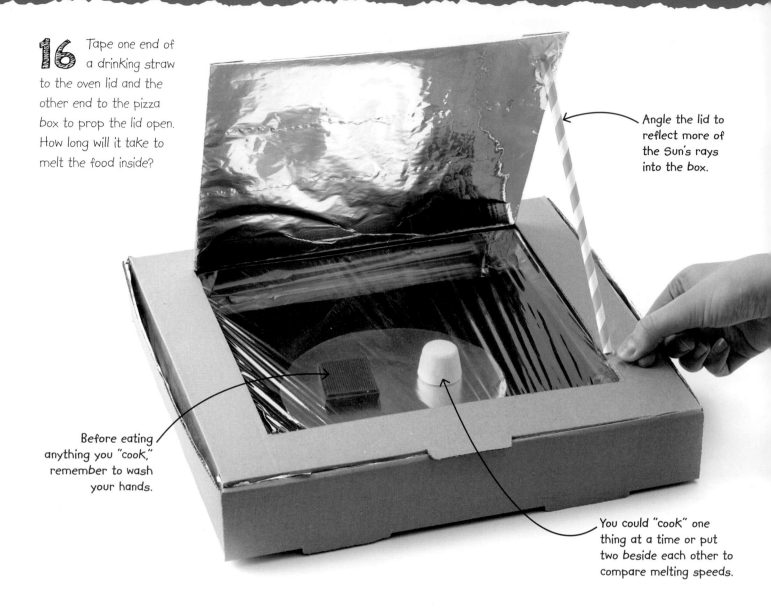

16 Tape one end of a drinking straw to the oven lid and the other end to the pizza box to prop the lid open. How long will it take to melt the food inside?

Angle the lid to reflect more of the Sun's rays into the box.

Before eating anything you "cook," remember to wash your hands.

You could "cook" one thing at a time or put two beside each other to compare melting speeds.

HOW IT WORKS

A solar oven works by capturing energy from sunlight (as well as invisible infrared heat rays) to heat up the surfaces inside it. This heat is then transferred into the food. The tilted lid reflects additional sunlight into the box to maximize the amount of energy harnessed. Meanwhile, the black base absorbs energy to heat up, too, and the plastic-wrap lid traps all that valuable heat inside the solar oven.

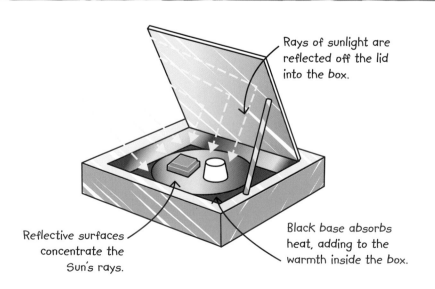

Rays of sunlight are reflected off the lid into the box.

Reflective surfaces concentrate the Sun's rays.

Black base absorbs heat, adding to the warmth inside the box.

THE SUN'S POWER

Every second, the Sun pumps out vast amounts of light and heat that spread in every direction. Only a tiny fraction of this falls onto Earth, about 93 million miles (150 million km) away, so imagine how hot the Sun itself must be. In fact, the Sun's surface is a searing 9,900°F (5,500°C), while its core is an amazing 27 million°F (15 million°C). These temperatures, plus the crush of immense pressure, force tiny particles in the core called hydrogen nuclei to collide, stick together, and release energy. This process, called nuclear fusion, is the power source of all stars, and even though it only happens in the core, there's enough fuel to keep the Sun shining for billions of years.

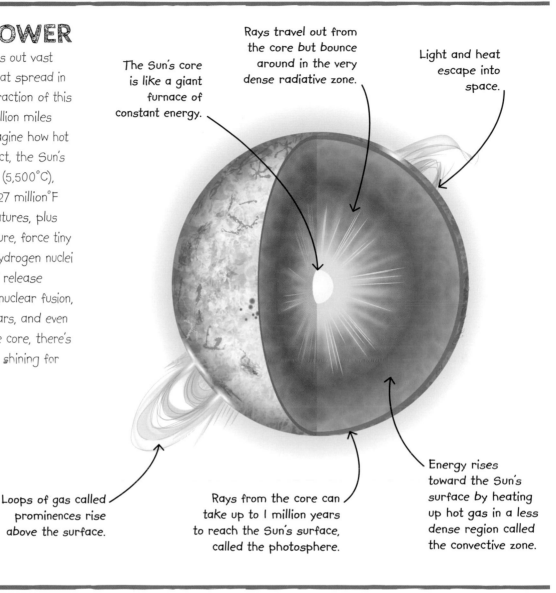

The Sun's core is like a giant furnace of constant energy.

Rays travel out from the core but bounce around in the very dense radiative zone.

Light and heat escape into space.

Loops of gas called prominences rise above the surface.

Rays from the core can take up to 1 million years to reach the Sun's surface, called the photosphere.

Energy rises toward the Sun's surface by heating up hot gas in a less dense region called the convective zone.

SPACE SCIENCE
HARNESSING THE SUN

Solar ovens are a great way to save energy and avoid using expensive and polluting fuels. In some sunny countries, the same principle is used for clean-energy power plants such as this one in Israel. Here, huge rings of mirrors (just like the reflective surfaces in your solar oven) direct sunlight onto a central "power tower" in which water is boiled and turned into steam. This steam in turn drives a generator to create electricity.

MAP THE PLANETS
3D SOLAR SYSTEM

The Sun sits at the center of a family of eight planets called the Solar System. Each one of these planets, including Earth, travels around the Sun on its own special path, or "orbit." This clever orrery will help you map the Solar System in three dimensions.

The Sun is a colossal ball of hot, electrically charged gas known as plasma.

Mercury is the smallest, innermost, and fastest-moving planet.

Earth is the only planet in the Solar System with liquid water and life on its surface.

Venus has the hottest surface of any planet thanks to an atmosphere that traps the Sun's heat.

Mars is a dry, cold, and dusty planet about half the size of Earth.

Jupiter is a vast ball of gas wrapped in colorful cloud bands, with a giant oval storm called the Great Red Spot.

Saturn is a gas giant planet surrounded by a beautiful system of rings made of countless chunks of rock and ice.

Uranus is made of icy slush and orbits the Sun tipped over on its side.

Neptune is the outermost planet, a blue ice giant with high winds and dark storms on its surface.

WHAT IS AN ORRERY?

A 3D model of the Solar System is called an "orrery." Scientists have built orreries for centuries to help them understand the paths taken by the planets and their changing positions.

MAKE YOUR OWN
ORRERY

This orrery has a cardstock base and cardstock arms that are all double-thickness for strength. The planets are made of modeling clay, with a ping-pong ball inside the Sun to make it lighter.

Time	**Difficulty**	**Warning**
2 hours	Medium	Be careful with cocktail sticks

WHAT YOU NEED

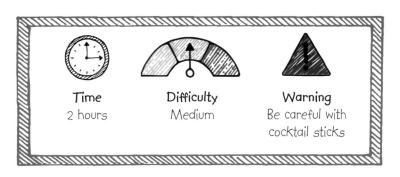

Stiff cardstock

White cardstock

Ruler

Pencil

Scissors

Paintbrush

Toothpicks

Ping-pong ball

White glue

Compass

4 in (10 cm) dowel

Thumb tack

Acrylic paints

Modeling clay

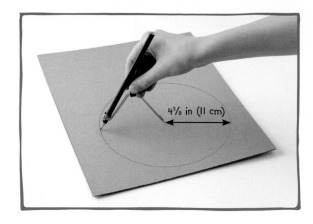

1 To make the base, set your compass to a radius of about 4³⁄₈ in (11 cm) and draw two circles onto stiff cardstock.

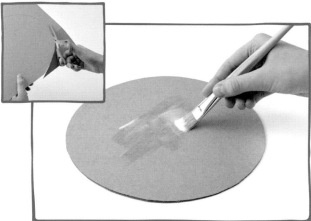

2 Cut out both circles. Apply glue to one side of a circle, then stick both circles together. This will make them stronger. Leave to set.

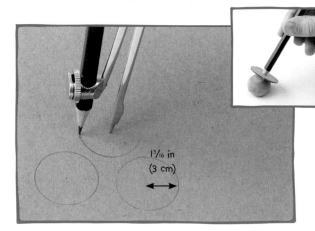

1³⁄₁₆ in (3 cm)

3 Draw three circles with a radius of 1³⁄₁₆ in (3 cm), then cut them out. Push a hole into the center of each one with a pencil. (Put a piece of modeling clay behind the cardstock for safety.)

4 Apply glue to one side of each circle and stick them in the middle of the large circle, one on top of the other.

Line up the holes so they are all on top of each other.

5 Once the glue is dry, paint the base with black paint. Leave to dry thoroughly. Apply a second coat of paint if it looks a bit patchy.

Make the Sun around 2⁹⁄₁₆ in (6.5 cm) in diameter.

The ping-pong ball makes your Sun weigh less.

6 Meanwhile, make your Sun. Wrap some modeling clay around a ping-pong ball, covering the ball completely to make a smooth sphere.

7 Next, make your planets. Start by rolling a piece of modeling clay in your hands into a ball the size of a golf ball for the largest planet, Jupiter.

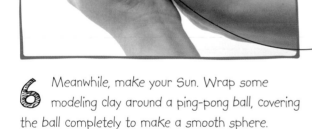

Sun | Mercury | Venus | Earth | Mars | Jupiter | Saturn | Uranus | Neptune

In reality, Jupiter, the biggest planet, is large enough to swallow 1,300 Earths.

9 Carefully insert one end of a toothpick into each of the clay balls.

8 Make the next balls as follows: one ping-pong-ball-sized (Saturn); two grape-sized (Uranus and Neptune); two marble-sized (Venus and Earth); one a bit smaller than a marble (Mars); and one even smaller again (Mercury).

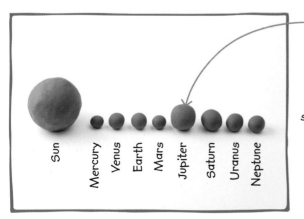

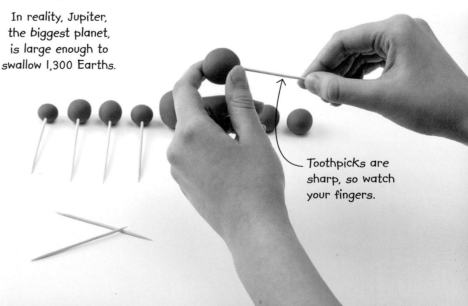

Toothpicks are sharp, so watch your fingers.

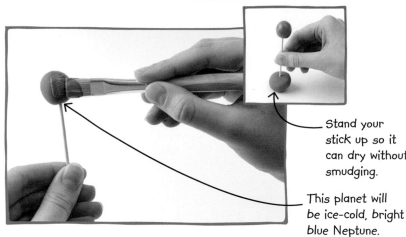

Stand your stick up so it can dry without smudging.

This planet will be ice-cold, bright blue Neptune.

10 Paint each ball to match its corresponding planet (see pages 30–31). Push the stick into some spare modeling clay and leave to dry.

11 Insert three toothpicks into the Sun to support it while you paint it. Use yellow, orange, red—any color that is fiery!

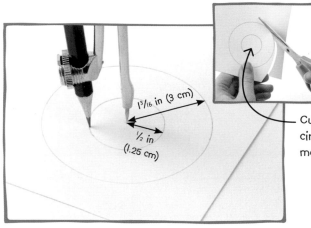

1³/₁₆ in (3 cm)

½ in (1.25 cm)

Cut the inner circle out to make a ring.

Saturn's solid-looking rings are really made of countless icy boulders orbiting the planet.

12 For Saturn's rings, draw two circles, one inside the other, on white cardstock: one with a 1³/₁₆ in (3 cm) radius and one with a ½ in (1.25 cm) radius. Cut them out.

13 Paint the ring on both sides with circles of pale yellow, pale brown, and gray, then position it at an angle on its clay ball.

These strips will be the "arms" of your orrery, holding the planets in position.

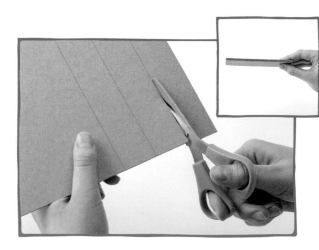

14 Cut eight strips 1³/₁₆ in (3 cm) wide, of these lengths: 11 in, 9½ in, 8¼ in, 6⁵/₁₆ in, 5⅛ in, 4⅜ in, 3⁹/₁₆ in, and 2¾ in (28 cm, 24 cm, 21 cm, 16 cm, 13 cm, 11 cm, 9 cm, and 7 cm).

15 Cut out the strips, then cut out a second set. Glue the pairs of strips back to back so they are all double-thickness. Leave to set.

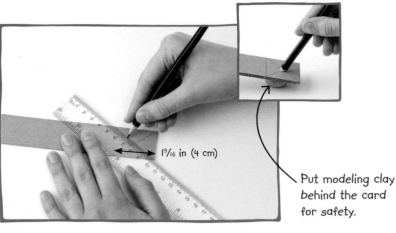

16 At one end of each strip, rule off a 1⁹⁄₁₆-in (4-cm) area. Draw diagonal lines across it to find the center. Make a hole there with a pencil.

Put modeling clay behind the card for safety.

17 Paint each strip with *black* paint on both sides and leave to dry. Apply a second coat if they don't seem quite dark enough.

18 Push the piece of dowel carefully into the clay Sun. Center it so that the weight is evenly balanced when you hold the stick upright.

The Sun is so big that 1.3 million Earths could fit inside it.

19 Slide the strips onto the dowel, threading them through the holes you made in Step 16. Add them in size order, starting with the smallest.

20 Continue until all the strips are on the dowel, finishing with the largest one. Check that they all rotate freely on the dowel.

Wiggle any strips that are tight on the dowel so they move freely.

21 Use a paintbrush to push some glue down into the hole in the middle of the base, ready to insert the dowel.

The influence of the Sun's gravity stretches across the Solar System, holding the planets in orbit around it.

22 Push the dowel into the hole and make sure it is sticking up straight. (Prop it up if you need to.) Leave to dry.

23 Use a thumb tack to make a small hole ⁹/₁₆ in (1.5 cm) from the outer end of each strip, placing a piece of modeling clay behind for safety.

Ask an adult for help snipping off the tips.

24 Start with the planet farthest from the Sun, Neptune. Carefully push its stick into the hole on the longest strip and snip off the tip on the underside.

Push each stick slightly farther through the strip, so the planets all end up level.

25 Continue adding the planets, trimming off the tips as you go. Once you have snipped off each tip, move its strip to align with the others and make sure the planets are all the same height.

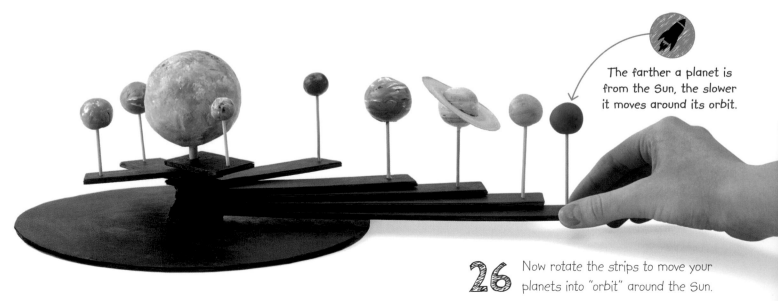

The farther a planet is from the Sun, the slower it moves around its orbit.

26 Now rotate the strips to move your planets into "orbit" around the Sun.

THE SOLAR SYSTEM

The rocky inner planets (Mercury, Venus, Earth, and Mars) are clustered near the Sun. Around them is a ring of space rocks called the asteroid belt. The outer planets (Jupiter, Saturn, Uranus, and Neptune) are mostly gas and icy slush. This diagram shows their sizes relative to Earth and the time (in Earth years) each one takes to orbit the Sun.

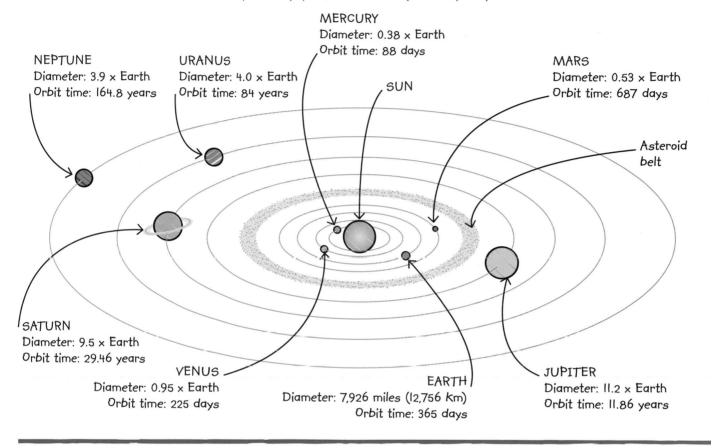

MERCURY
Diameter: 0.38 × Earth
Orbit time: 88 days

NEPTUNE
Diameter: 3.9 × Earth
Orbit time: 164.8 years

URANUS
Diameter: 4.0 × Earth
Orbit time: 84 years

SUN

MARS
Diameter: 0.53 × Earth
Orbit time: 687 days

Asteroid belt

SATURN
Diameter: 9.5 × Earth
Orbit time: 29.46 years

VENUS
Diameter: 0.95 × Earth
Orbit time: 225 days

EARTH
Diameter: 7,926 miles (12,756 km)
Orbit time: 365 days

JUPITER
Diameter: 11.2 × Earth
Orbit time: 11.86 years

SPACE SCIENCE
MODEL SOLAR SYSTEMS

People first made 3D models to show the movements of the planets in ancient Greece more than 2,000 years ago, but the first orreries were invented in the early 1700s. By this time, astronomers had realized that the Sun, rather than Earth, was the center of the Solar System. These models, such as this pre-1781 antique orrery, usually contained clockwork mechanisms to keep all the planets orbiting at the right speeds in relation to each other.

This model includes the five moons known for Saturn at the time, but in fact the planet has more than 80 moons.

This orrery doesn't include the planets Uranus and Neptune, as they hadn't been discovered when it was made.

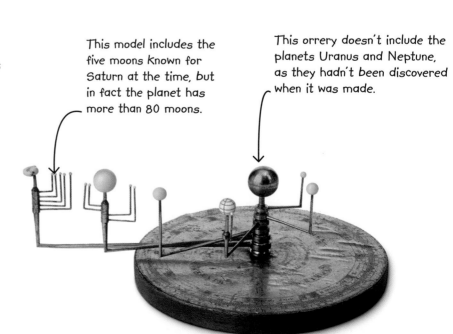

CAPTURE THE LIGHT
PINHOLE CAMERA

Looking directly at the Sun is dangerous—including through binoculars or a telescope—so how can you watch the Sun's activity without risking your eyesight? The solution is to make this pinhole camera, which creates an image of the Sun you can safely observe.

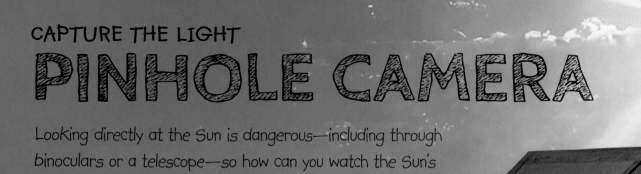

Point the camera at the Sun and see an upside-down image of it appear on this screen.

Seal the box and paint it black inside and out to keep out all light and reflections.

WHAT MIGHT YOU SEE?

A pinhole camera is a great (and safe!) way to view the Sun's activities, such as solar eclipses—rare events when the Moon blocks out part or all of the Sun's light (see page 41). It's also a good way to see sunspots, which are dark patches of cool gas on the Sun's surface that can grow to the size of planets.

MAKE YOUR OWN
PINHOLE CAMERA

For this project, you adapt a shoebox to exclude light, then make a pinprick at one end. This tiny hole lets in light that is then projected onto a screen at the other end of the box.

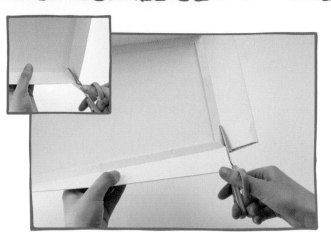

Time	Difficulty	Warning
45 minutes	Easy	Never look directly at the Sun

WHAT YOU NEED

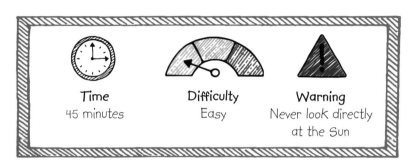

Ruler

Pencil

Tracing paper

Black acrylic paint

Thumb tack

Scissors

Masking tape

Paintbrush

White glue

Shoebox

1 To make the lid, cut into each corner of the shoebox lid to flatten the sides, then cut off the sides to leave a flat rectangle of cardstock.

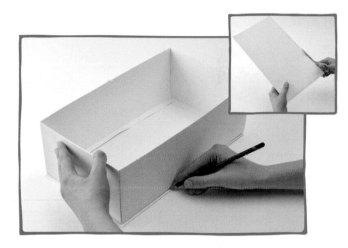

2 Place the shoebox on the lid and draw around it. Trim the lid along the lines you've drawn so it's exactly the same size as the box.

3 On one end of the shoebox, mark a border ¾ in (2 cm) from all four edges. Join the marks to draw a rectangle.

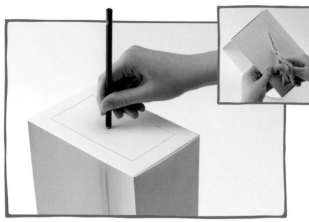

This rectangular opening will form a viewing screen for your camera.

4 Make a hole with a pencil inside the rectangle, then push your scissors into the hole and cut out a rectangular opening.

5 Paint the side of the shoebox black around the opening, then paint the entire inside of the box black, plus one side of the lid. Leave to dry.

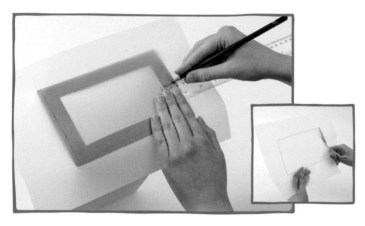

6 For the screen, measure a piece of tracing paper to fit over the opening with a border of 9/16 in (1.5 cm). Cut the tracing paper to size.

7 Glue all four edges of the screen flat onto the inside of the box, over the opening. Press until the glue has set.

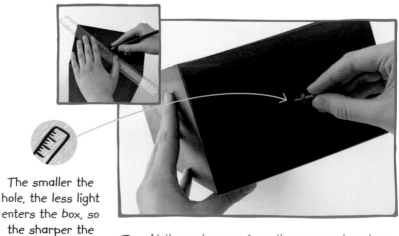

The smaller the hole, the less light enters the box, so the sharper the image on the screen.

8 Tape the lid onto the box, black side facing inward, leaving no gaps through which light can enter. Paint the outside of the box black.

9 At the end across from the screen, draw two lines from corner to corner. Where they cross, at the center, make a hole with a thumb tack.

The light through the pinhole will project an upside-down image of the Sun on this screen.

Black absorbs light, so it is not reflected inside the box, keeping the Sun's image sharp.

The pinhole will let in a tiny amount of light.

10 Point the box toward the Sun (but never look directly at it). You'll see the image of the Sun appear on your screen.

HOW IT WORKS

The front of the pinhole camera blocks all the Sun's rays except the ones whose paths pass through the pinhole. Once inside the camera, these rays spread out again to form an image on the screen. Because the rays crossed over at the pinhole, the image you will see on the back screen is upside down.

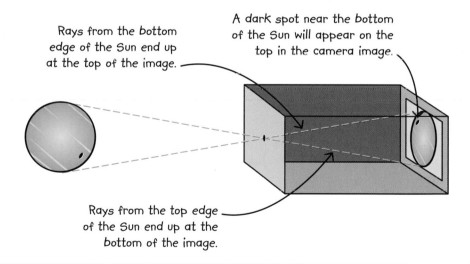

Rays from the bottom edge of the Sun end up at the top of the image.

A dark spot near the bottom of the Sun will appear on the top in the camera image.

Rays from the top edge of the Sun end up at the bottom of the image.

SPACE SCIENCE
WHAT IS AN ECLIPSE?

A solar eclipse happens when the Moon's orbit takes it in front of the Sun as seen from a part of Earth's surface, so that its disk casts a shadow and blocks all or part of the Sun's light from reaching this area. They only occur when Earth, the Moon, and the Sun all line up. A lunar eclipse is also possible (see pages 152–153).

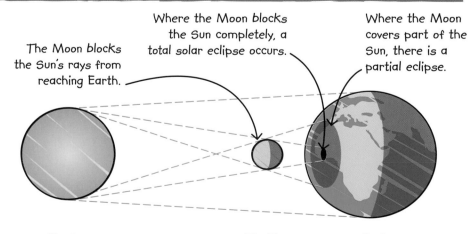

The Moon blocks the Sun's rays from reaching Earth.

Where the Moon blocks the Sun completely, a total solar eclipse occurs.

Where the Moon covers part of the Sun, there is a partial eclipse.

The Sun   The Moon   Earth

HOW FAR? HOW LONG?
GRAVITY EXPERIMENT

Gravity is what keeps us on the ground and keeps Earth on its orbit around the Sun. But how does it work? Build this catapult to experiment with gravity and see what impact it has on objects with different masses.

WHAT IS GRAVITY?
Gravity is a force that pulls objects toward each other. The bigger an object's mass (the more stuff it contains) and the closer you get to it, the stronger the pull. This pull of gravity on objects with mass is the effect we know as weight.

The catapult uses energy stored in the stretched rubber band (its "potential energy") to fire each object into the air.

Use objects of a similar size but different mass, then compare how far they travel.

Place a tape measure on the ground to record how far the balls travel.

MAKE YOUR OWN
CATAPULT

Build this simple catapult, then use it to experiment with balls of the same size but different mass. Ask an adult where to do it, as the balls may go farther than you expect!

Time	Difficulty	Warning
30 mins	Easy	Ask an adult where you can safely do this experiment

WHAT YOU NEED

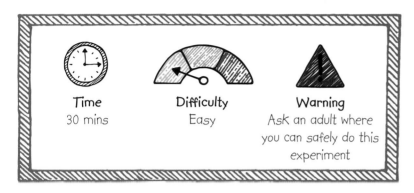

Ruler

Pencil

Dowel 2 in (5 cm) long

Duct tape

Scales

2 dowels 9¾ in (25 cm) long

Tape measure

Balls of the same size but different masses

Notebook

Long rubber band

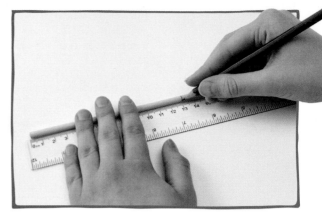

1 Make a mark on each of the two long dowels 5⅛ in (13 cm) from one end.

2 Cut an 7-in (18-cm) piece of duct tape and lay it sticky-side up on a work surface. Position the small dowel in the middle of its length and close to one edge of the tape.

3 Place the two long dowels at either end of the small dowel, lining it up with the pencil marks. Position the dowels so that they cross at one end, as shown.

At this point, the two dowels are still crossed over each other.

4 Fold one end of the tape over the long dowel and up to rest on the small dowel. Then fold the other end over the other long dowel.

5 Fold the two ends of the tape over the top of the small dowel and press to stick everything firmly together.

The two sticks are now tensioned against each other, storing potential energy.

6 Ease open the two long dowels to uncross them. Line them up side by side and secure in place with another strip of duct tape.

7 Wrap tape around the lower section of the dowels, then stick a piece of tape up one side, through the middle, and back down the other side.

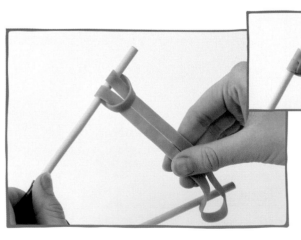

The taped area is the handle of your catapult.

8 Fold the rubber band back on itself to make a loop in it, thread one end of a dowel through the loop, and pull the rubber band tight.

9 Repeat Step 8 at the other end of the rubber band for the other dowel. Pull tight, then your catapult is ready for the experiment.

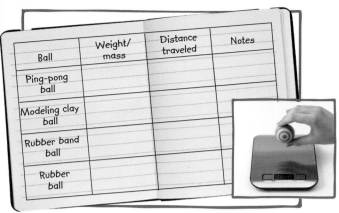

Ball	Weight/ mass	Distance traveled	Notes
Ping-pong ball			
Modeling clay ball			
Rubber band ball			
Rubber ball			

10 Make a chart to record how far each ball travels when you release the catapult. Weigh each ball and log the values in the chart.

11 Lay out a tape measure to record how far the balls fly, and stand at the beginning of it. Fire each ball out of the catapult, trying to apply the same amount of "ping" every time. Record your findings.

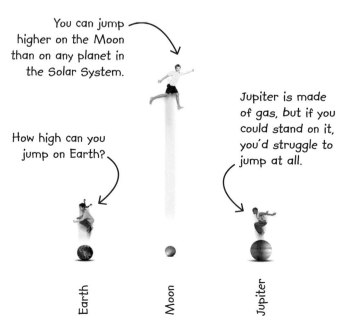

Stretching the rubber band stores potential energy; when you let go, the energy is released and the ball will fly.

Aim in the same direction each time, from the same height.

Hold the handle with one hand and put the ball into the catapult. Pull back, aim, and fire!

HOW IT WORKS

Gravity pulls objects downward. This force is the same whatever an object's mass, so the balls should all travel the same distance before gravity pulls them to the ground. But some balls travel farther. Why is that? It's due to air resistance—air pushes back at each ball with the same force, but it can slow down a light ping-pong ball more easily than a heavy golf ball.

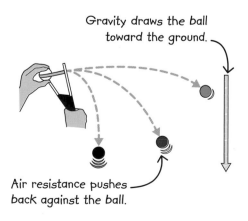

Gravity draws the ball toward the ground.

Air resistance pushes back against the ball.

SPACE SCIENCE
DIFFERENCES IN GRAVITY

Across the Solar System, the moons and planets have different strengths of gravity. On the Moon, gravity is just one-sixth of Earth's; on Jupiter, it's so strong that it would be hard to lift your feet at all.

You can jump higher on the Moon than on any planet in the Solar System.

How high can you jump on Earth?

Jupiter is made of gas, but if you could stand on it, you'd struggle to jump at all.

Earth   Moon   Jupiter

TWINKLE, TWINKLE, LOTS OF STARS
CONSTELLATION LAMPSHADE

Bring the night sky into your bedroom with this star-spangled lampshade. There are billions of stars in the sky, which astronomers have organized into constellations, each with their own name. Which ones will you choose to twinkle brightly by your bedside?

WHAT ARE CONSTELLATIONS?

Constellations are groups of stars that can be seen from Earth. There are 88 constellations that fit together like a jigsaw puzzle to cover the entire sky (see pages 147–149).

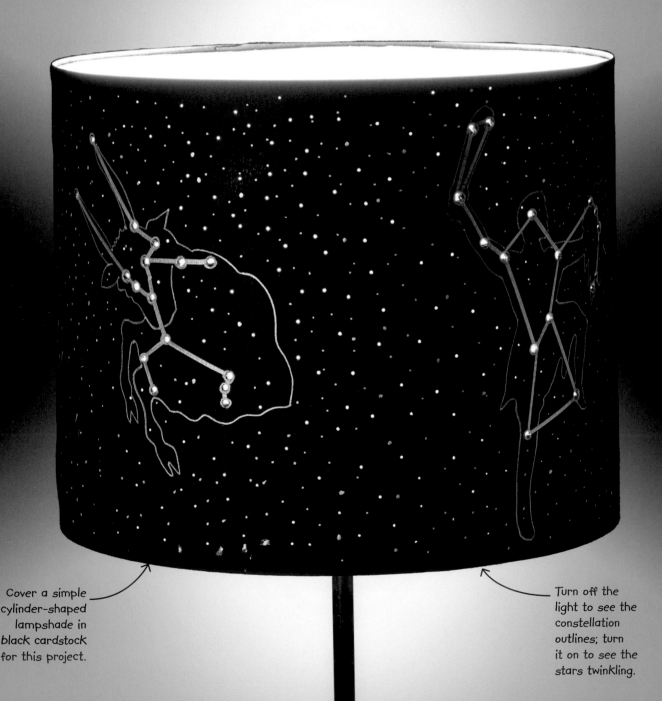

Cover a simple cylinder-shaped lampshade in black cardstock for this project.

Turn off the light to see the constellation outlines; turn it on to see the stars twinkling.

MAKE YOUR OWN
STARSHADE

Choose whichever constellations you want for this project, from a book or the internet—you could research ones from different cultures, too. Depending on the size of your lampshade, you will probably need 4–5 constellations in total.

Time	**Difficulty**	**Warning**
1½ hours	Easy	Ask an adult to fit the shade to the lamp

WHAT YOU NEED

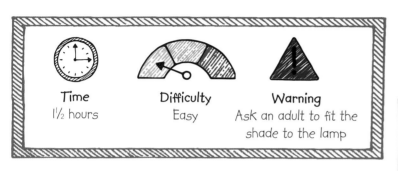

Ruler

Masking tape

Scissors

Pencil

Tape measure

Thick and thin silver markers

Thumb tack

White glue

Gold marker

Corrugated cardboard

Tracing paper

Black cardstock

Lamp and cylinder-shaped lampshade

1 Measure the height and circumference of the lampshade. To allow for overlap, add ¾ in (2 cm) to the circumference.

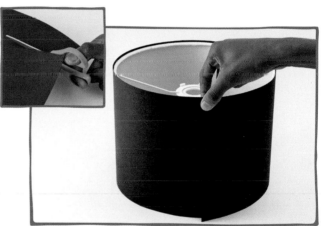

2 Transfer the measurements onto black cardstock, then cut out the rectangle and check it fits around the lampshade.

Mark each star in a constellation with a small circle.

3 Trace the outline of each constellation and its stars onto tracing paper. Flip the tracing paper over and draw over the lines again.

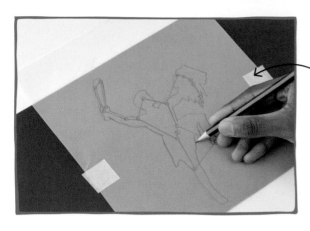

Use masking tape to hold the tracing paper in place as you draw.

4 Turn the tracing paper back over, and pencil over each shape again to transfer it onto the black cardstock.

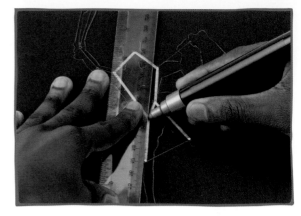

5 Using a thick silver marker and a ruler, carefully draw over the trace marks to join the circles of the individual stars within the constellations.

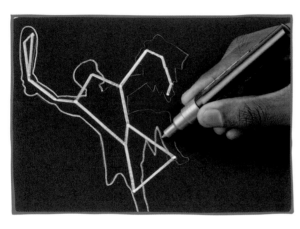

6 Next, use a thick gold marker to draw over the pencil outlines you traced of each constellation's shape.

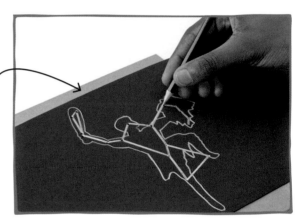

Put corrugated cardboard behind the black card to protect the surface under it.

7 Push a pencil through each of the circles that mark where a star is to make a small hole inside each circle.

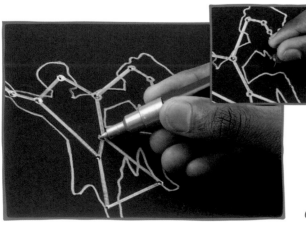

8 Draw a small circle with a thin silver marker around each star hole, then use a thumb tack to prick random holes all over the cardstock.

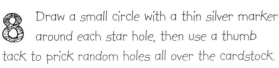

There are about 6,000 stars bright enough to see from Earth with just your eyes.

9 With the thin silver marker, add dots between the holes. These are your daytime stars, when the light is off; the holes are stars by night, when it is on.

Stars are huge, distant balls of gas that generate heat and light.

Every star and other object in the sky is part of a constellation.

10 Paint glue along the top and bottom of the cardstock, stick it to the shade, and hold until set. Ask an adult to fit the shade on the lamp. Now you have a "night sky" by day or night!

SPACE SCIENCE
CONSTELLATION NAMES

How do constellations get their names? Since prehistoric times, people have seen patterns, or constellations, in some of the brightest stars and named them after objects or creatures. Although these constellations often involved the same stars, people in different cultures gave them their own names—for instance, Indian astronomers saw a crocodile where European ones saw the goat-fish Capricornus. Sometimes the same constellation was invented separately in different cultures.

The constellation Orion is recognized as a hunter in both Indigenous Australian cultures and in Europe.

Both the Mi'kmaq First Nations People of Canada and the ancient Greeks saw the figure of a great bear in the constellation Ursa Major.

What Greek astronomers named Capricornus was Maraka, the crocodile, for Indian astronomers.

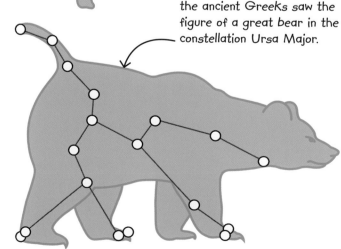

PLANET ON A PLATE
EARTH CAKE

The outer crust of our planet hides three main layers—
a mantle, an outer core, and an inner core—and so does
the icing layer of this cake. Follow the steps of this
project to bake your own multilayered Earth cake.

This project makes a half-
sphere cake, but if you want,
make two cakes and stick them
together for a whole Earth.

Copy the shapes
of the continents
from a book or
print them off
the internet.

Our planet is 7,918 miles
(12,742 km) in diameter, but
this cake will fit on
a dinner plate.

INSIDE EARTH

Earth formed out of colliding space rocks 4.5 billion years ago that were hot enough to melt together. Gravity pulled the heavy elements into the center to form a core that is still largely molten today. Over time, Earth gradually cooled and solidified into layers (see page 57), with a rocky crust capped by oceans and land.

Make the land masses of islands and continents with green icing.

Use blue icing for water, which covers most of the planet.

Slice into the cake to see layers of color, just like the layers of Earth.

MAKE YOUR OWN
PLANET CAKE

This recipe makes a hemisphere—a half-sphere—but at least it won't roll off the plate! For a full planet, bake two hemispheres and stick them together with warmed jam.

Time	Difficulty	Warning
3 hours, including cooling time	Medium	Ask an adult to help you use the oven

WHAT YOU NEED

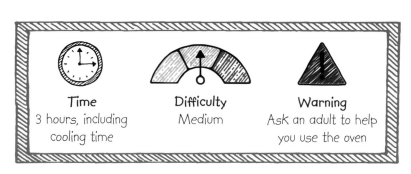

4 in (10 cm), 7 in (8 cm), and 8½ in (22 cm) hemisphere cake pans

Rolling pin

Wooden spoon

Pencil

Cooling rack

Small bowl

2 tbsp jam

Powdered sugar

Pastry brush

Scissors

Small, medium, and large mixing bowls

11¾ oz (335 g) all-purpose flour

11¾ oz (335 g) sugar

11¾ oz (335 g) butter, softened

Blue and green fondant icing

Red, orange, and yellow food coloring

Tracing paper

Baking sheet

Modeling tool

Palette knife

Tablespoon

Skewer or toothpick

Baking ring

6 medium eggs

Spatula

Paintbrush

1 First, wash your hands thoroughly, then grease the cake pans with soft butter and dust them with flour to prevent the cakes from sticking to them.

2 In the largest mixing bowl, stir the sugar and butter together with the wooden spoon, beating until the mixture is fluffy.

3 Add one egg and beat it thoroughly into the mixture. Repeat to add each of the eggs, one by one, and mixing well each time.

Divide the mixture approximately; you don't have to be too precise.

4 Gently stir in the flour. Fold it into the mixture until everything is thoroughly combined together.

5 Leave half of the mixture in the large bowl. Split the other half so that about two-thirds is in a medium bowl and one-third in a small bowl.

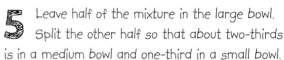

Keep adding drops of color until it's as bright as you'd like it.

6 Add some yellow food coloring to the small bowl and stir it thoroughly but gently into the mixture until well combined.

7 Repeat Step 6 to add orange food coloring to the mixture in the medium-sized bowl and then red to the mixture in the large bowl.

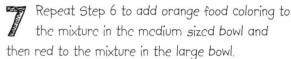

The inner core of Earth is 1,700 miles (2,740 km) across.

8 Your three different-colored cake mixes are now ready to transfer into the cake pans, so preheat the oven to 350°F (180°C).

9 Put the yellow mixture into the smallest of the three cake pans you prepared in Step 1 and level it off.

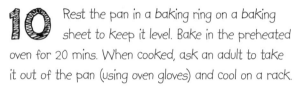

To test if your cake is cooked, insert a skewer or toothpick: if it comes out clean, the cake's ready; if not, bake a bit longer.

10 Rest the pan in a baking ring on a baking sheet to keep it level. Bake in the preheated oven for 20 mins. When cooked, ask an adult to take it out of the pan (using oven gloves) and cool on a rack.

11 Meanwhile, put the orange cake mix into the medium-sized cake pan. With a tablespoon, scoop out a "well" in the center.

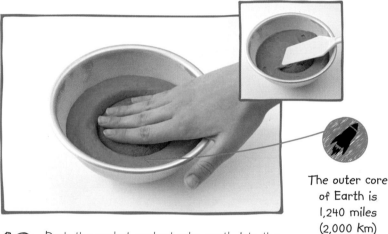

The outer core of Earth is 1,240 miles (2,000 km) thick.

12 Push the cooled, cooked cake gently into the well, dome-side down, so it sits below the surface. Level off the orange mixture to cover it.

13 Bake in the oven for about 30 mins. As in Step 10, test with a skewer or toothpick to make sure it is cooked, then let it cool on a wire rack.

Ease the cooked cake down into the well, dome-side down.

14 Put the red mixture into the largest cake pan. Make another well in the center and gently push the cooled, cooked cake into it.

15 When the cooked cake is sitting just below the surface of the red mixture, smooth the mixture level over the cooked cake.

Earth's mantle is 1,800 miles (2,900 km) thick.

16 Bake for about 40 mins, then test with a skewer or toothpick to ensure it's cooked (see Step 10) before letting it cool on a wire rack.

17 Turn the cake dome-side down. Ask an adult to help you carefully level off the *base* with a palette knife, so the cake sits flat on a plate.

Lightly dust the work surface with powdered sugar to keep the icing from sticking to it.

The sticky jam will "glue" the icing layer to the cooked cake.

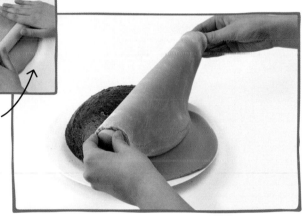

18 Thin the jam with a tablespoon of hot water. Brush the dome of the cake with a coating of jam.

19 Roll out the *blue* icing until it is large enough to cover the cake and ¼ in (5 mm) thick. Use the rolling pin to lift the icing onto the cake.

Use tracing paper to copy the shapes of the land masses.

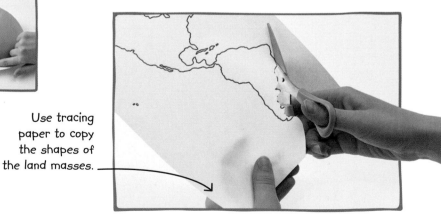

20 Smooth the icing down to the base of the cake. Cut away the excess with a modeling tool and neaten the edge with your finger.

21 Which part of the world will you put on your cake? Trace the shapes from a *book* or the internet and cut out the areas of land.

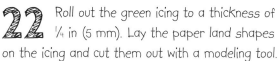

You don't need to be too neat—just follow the basic outlines.

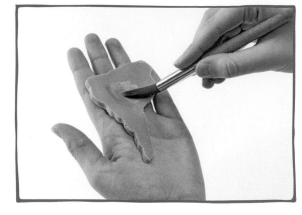

22 Roll out the green icing to a thickness of ¼ in (5 mm). Lay the paper land shapes on the icing and cut them out with a modeling tool.

23 Turn each land shape over and paint the back of it with a little water to make it stick to the blue icing.

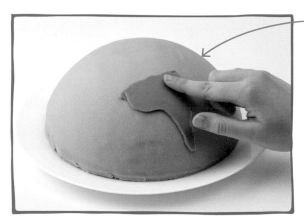

Earth's outer crust is a thin layer 50 miles (80 km) thick.

24 Carefully position the land shapes on the cake and gently press them down with your finger.

25 Once you have all your land shapes in position, smooth the edges with your modeling tool to neaten them.

BEYOND EARTH ...

Every planet in our Solar System looks very different both inside and out (see pages 30–31), and you could bake cakes of some of Earth's neighbors, too. Color the layers differently and decorate to match the surface of each moon or planet—maybe add some edible glitter, make dimpled craters, or swirl colored icing to create bands of clouds.

Create a Moon cake with a rough, rocky gray buttercream surface and circles of fondant icing for craters.

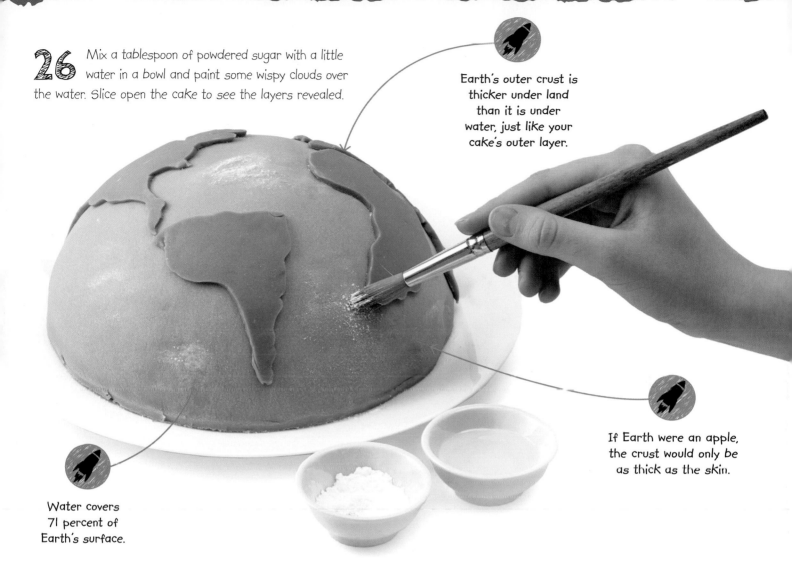

26 Mix a tablespoon of powdered sugar with a little water in a bowl and paint some wispy clouds over the water. Slice open the cake to see the layers revealed.

Earth's outer crust is thicker under land than it is under water, just like your cake's outer layer.

If Earth were an apple, the crust would only be as thick as the skin.

Water covers 71 percent of Earth's surface.

SPACE SCIENCE
THE LAYERS OF EARTH

Earth's outer layer is the crust, which is made of soil and rock. Beneath that, the middle layer—the mantle—is hot, partially molten rock that churns very slowly, pulling the crust in different directions and causing earthquakes. The inner layer, or core, of Earth has two parts—an outer core of thick liquid rock and a solid inner core.

Made of solid iron and nickel, the inner core is as hot as the surface of the Sun.

The outer core is liquid metal.

The force of gravity pulls Earth into an almost perfect sphere.

The thick mantle layer is mostly dense silicate rock, rich in iron and magnesium.

Earth's crust is a thin layer of rock.

STARBURSTS AND SPACE CLOUDS
GALAXY GALLERY

Think the universe is just a big empty space? Far from it! It's scattered with billions of galaxies of different shapes and sizes, such as spiral, elliptical, and irregular. When seen through a telescope, they are incredibly beautiful—and inspiration for this fun art project.

Irregular galaxies are shapeless, with bright young stars, so this random sponging technique works well.

WHAT IS A GALAXY?

Galaxies are huge clouds of stars, gas, and dust held together by their own gravity. Some have only a few million stars in them, but others—like our own Milky Way Galaxy (see pages 146-147)—are giant spirals or balls containing many billions of stars. All the stars you can see in the sky are part of the Milky Way Galaxy.

Some large galaxies have long spiral arms packed with newborn stars. Swirl soft pastels into a beautiful, interlocking spiral.

Spiral galaxies look different depending on our viewpoint. Water-soluble pencils work well for this spiral galaxy viewed almost edge-on.

SPACE SCIENCE
TYPES OF GALAXIES

Galaxies come in many types, from balls of faint red and yellow stars called ellipticals to shapeless clouds of bright blue and white stars called irregulars. Our own Milky Way is a "barred spiral." From our position between two of its spiral arms, it looks like a band of star clouds wrapping around the whole sky.

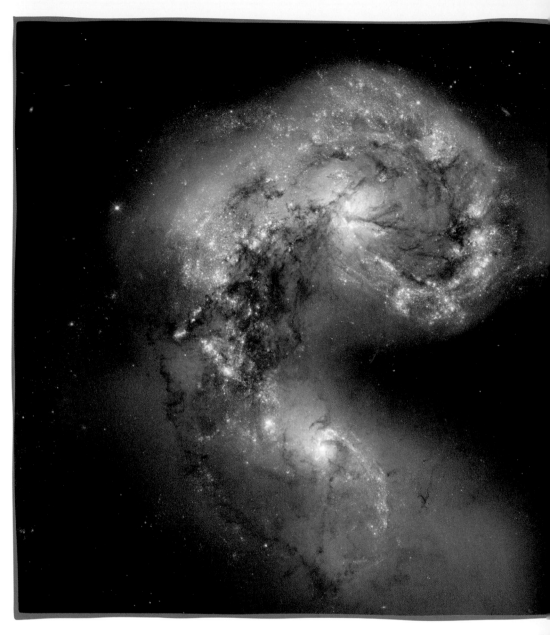

COLLIDING GALAXIES

Galaxies grow by colliding and merging together. This collision between two spiral galaxies has altered their shapes and triggered waves of star formation.

IRREGULAR
Shapeless galaxies that are rich in gas clouds that create bright new stars.

ELLIPTICAL
Huge balls of stars with a wide range of shapes, from perfect spheres to long, thin cylinders.

SPIRAL
Galaxies that have a central ball of stars, with spiral arms wrapping around it.

BARRED SPIRAL
Spiral arms enclose a central ball of stars with a straight bar emerging from each end.

LENTICULAR
Unusual galaxies that are like spiral galaxies without the bright arms.

MAKE YOUR OWN
SPACE ART

Just as galaxies are formed in different ways, these art projects use a variety of techniques and styles. Try these versions, then experiment some more—there are lots of other beautiful space formations you could create, too.

Time
1 hour

Difficulty
Easy

WHAT YOU NEED

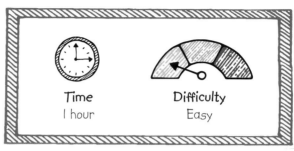

Paintbrushes

Silver marker

Black paper

Chalk pastels

Natural sponge

White paint mixed with a few drops of water

Bowl to use for dipping sponge into paint

Water-soluble pencils

Acrylic paints

Old toothbrush

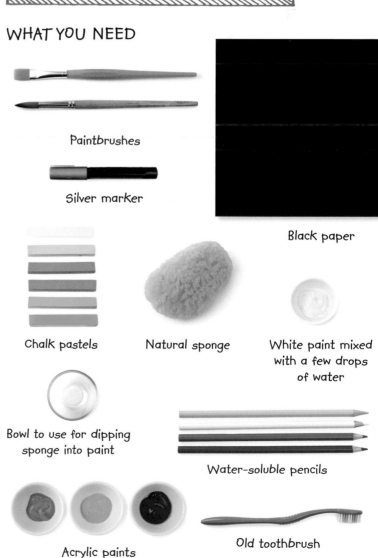

USING CHALK PASTELS

Keep your hand off the paper to avoid smudging the pastels.

1 Using a pink pastel, start in the center of the card and draw two overlapping spirals. Reinforce the lines, then repeat using a *blue* pastel instead.

2 Continue to build up your spirals and begin adding other colors, too, such as yellow and white.

USING A SPONGE

Keep the paint blobs scattered at the edges but more dense in the center.

1 Dip a sponge into different shades of *blue* paint and gently dab the cardstock with the colors to make a loose diagonal shape.

2 Next, dab on a few areas of *black*, followed by turquoise and lilac. Let the shape have rough edges and cloudlike wisps.

USING WATER-SOLUBLE PENCILS

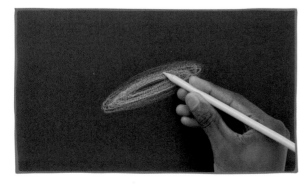

Stars in the middle of a spiral galaxy are so tightly packed, they blend into a blurry cloud.

1 Beginning with a *yellow* pencil, draw a rough oval shape. Let the pencil follow the shape to fill it loosely with color.

2 Fill in the center with a *white* pencil, then return to the edge, drawing loose, rough ovals in a *red* color.

Many galaxies develop two spiral arms as they grow, but some only have one arm.

3 Use a finger to gently smudge the colors. Follow the shape of the spirals, blending the colors and going out to the edges of the cardstock.

4 Dip an old toothbrush into the watery white paint. Flick the bristles to spray "stars" on your drawing. Leave to dry.

Irregular galaxies contain lots of young stars and dust.

3 Use both ends of the sponge and dab it in a mixture of colors to create random patterns on the cardstock.

4 Dip a paintbrush into diluted white paint. Hold it over the cardstock and gently tap it to splatter "stars" on your painting.

Use a clean paintbrush with just a little water on it.

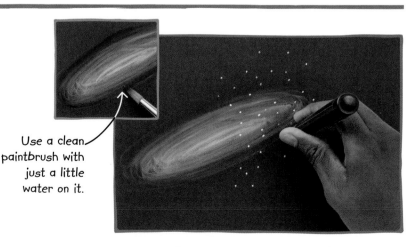

3 Add lines of pink and orange, too, keeping things denser in the center and more open toward the outer edge of the shape.

4 Gently stroke water over the oval to blend the colors. Once dry, use a silver marker to add random dots for the "stars."

SPACE EXPLORATION

How do we know what we know about space? It's thanks to all the rockets and rovers and probes and people who have gone into space and explored it. In this chapter, you'll build rockets, a space station, and a lunar rover to help you understand the incredible technology invented for space exploration. Make the helmet and oxygen tanks to examine how astronauts stay safe in space, and test your skills for the challenges of space—how to land a spacecraft, for instance, and how to dock with a space station.

WE HAVE LIFT-OFF!

ROCKET STOMPER

It takes an enormous amount of power and speed for rockets to escape Earth's gravity and fly into space, but make this rocket and launchpad and you are the power source. Take it outside and let the countdown commence ...

LAUNCH INTO SPACE

Rockets lift off vertically (straight up), then tilt as they gain speed until they are moving in line with the curve of Earth's surface. With enough speed, this lets them reach an orbit where they won't fall back to Earth.

The rocket is sent flying upwards by the incoming air.

Air is forced up into the rocket at speed when you stomp on the plastic bottle.

The tube drives air up into the body of the rocket.

MAKE YOUR OWN
ROCKET AND LAUNCHPAD

This clever rocket is powered by the air you push out of a plastic bottle when you stomp on it. And the best bit? Blow down the tube to reinflate the bottle and do it again ...

Time
2½ hours

Difficulty
Medium

Warning
Launch your rocket outside, not indoors

WHAT YOU NEED

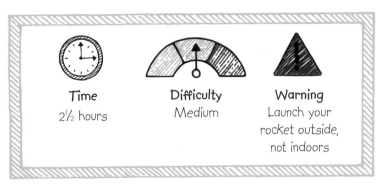

Ruler

Pencil

White cardstock

Stiff cardstock

Scissors

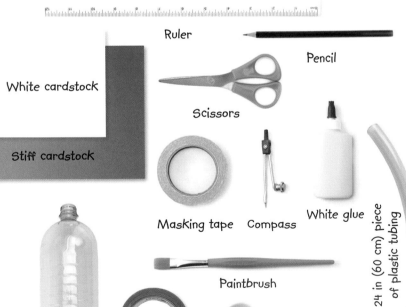

Masking tape   Compass

White glue

24 in (60 cm) piece of plastic tubing

Paintbrush

Duct tape

Black paint

Empty 2-liter plastic soda bottle

Washi tape in silver and other colors

Empty tissue box

MAKE THE ROCKET

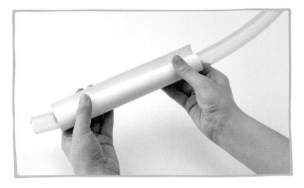

1 Cut a piece of white cardstock 8¼ in x 4¾ in (21 cm x 12 cm). Line up the long sides parallel with the tubing and roll the card snugly around it.

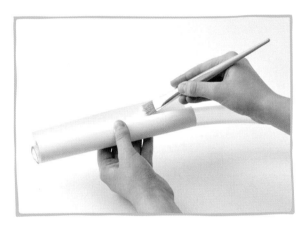

2 Glue along the cardstock edge, roll it up to seal the cylinder, and hold until set. Slide out the tubing, then measure the diameter of the cylinder.

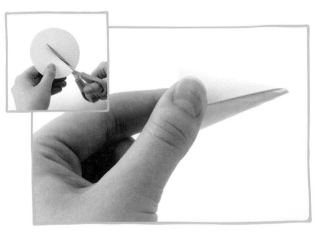

3 Make a white cardstock circle with a 1¾ in (4.5 cm) radius. Cut it in half. Glue one half into a cone, with a base the same diameter as the cylinder.

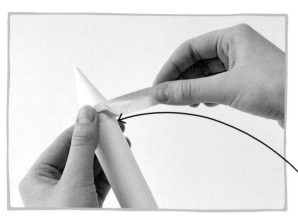

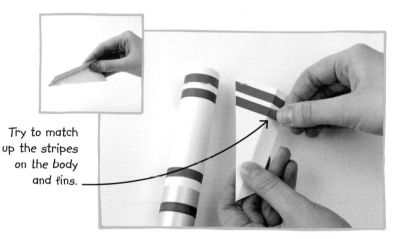

Check that your stripes join up neatly around the body.

Make a tight seal on the join so no air can escape.

4 Put the cone over one end of the cylinder and secure in place with a strip of silver washi tape. Press all the edges down to seal it.

5 Decorate the body of your rocket however you wish. We've used red, blue, and silver strips of washi tape.

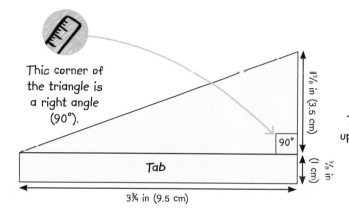

This corner of the triangle is a right angle (90°).

1⅜ in (3.5 cm)

90°

⅜ in (1 cm)

Tab

3¾ in (9.5 cm)

Try to match up the stripes on the body and fins.

6 Draw and cut out two right-angled triangles of white cardstock 1⅜ in (3.5 cm) high by 3¾ in (9.5 cm) long. Add a ⅜ in (1 cm) tab on the long edges.

7 Bend the two tabs to make fins for your rocket. (Hold a ruler on the line for a sharp crease.) Decorate them to match the rocket body.

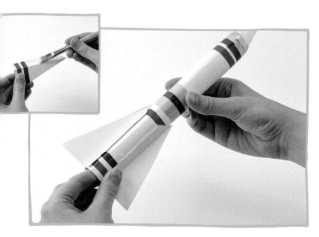

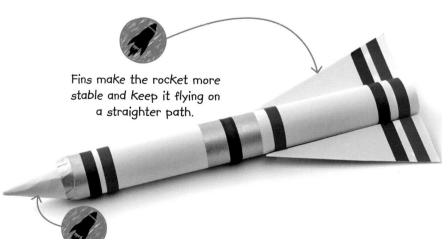

Fins make the rocket more stable and keep it flying on a straighter path.

Cone-shaped nose helps reduce drag from air as the rocket pushes forward.

8 Apply glue to the tabs on the two fins and stick them firmly onto either side of the rocket body, lining up the stripes if you can.

9 Put the rocket to one side to let the glue set thoroughly while you make your launcher.

MAKE THE LAUNCHER

Mark off a strip of card the same depth as the box.

1 Lay the tissue box on its side along one edge of the stiff cardstock. Draw a line along the edge of the box to mark off its depth.

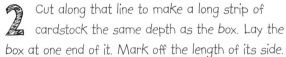

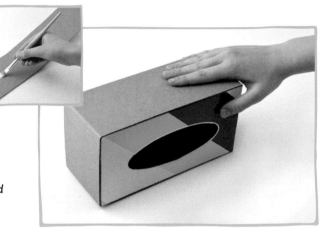

2 Cut along that line to make a long strip of cardstock the same depth as the box. Lay the box at one end of it. Mark off the length of its side.

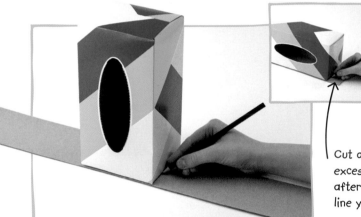

Cut away any excess card after the third line you drew.

3 Place the next side of the box at the line you drew in Step 2 and draw another line. Repeat for the third side, too, then cut along that third line.

4 Bend the cardstock along each of the two other lines you have drawn, then glue the strip to three sides of the box to reinforce it.

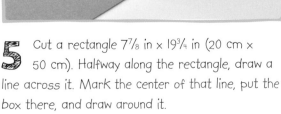

Line up the uncovered end of your box with the $9\frac{7}{8}$ in (25 cm) line.

5 Cut a rectangle $7\frac{7}{8}$ in x $19\frac{3}{4}$ in (20 cm x 50 cm). Halfway along the rectangle, draw a line across it. Mark the center of that line, put the box there, and draw around it.

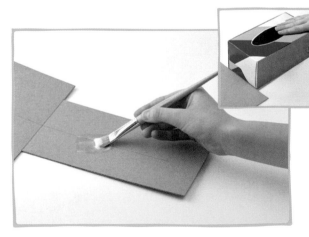

6 Cut out the area marked out by the box, up to the halfway line. Paint the area with glue and stick it firmly to the back of the box.

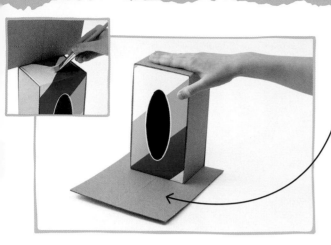

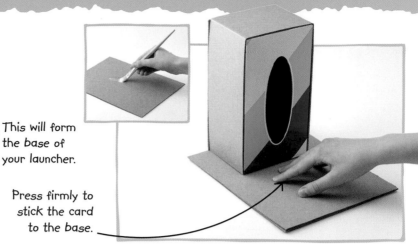

This will form the base of your launcher.

Press firmly to stick the card to the base.

7 Apply glue to the uncovered end of the box. Fold the cardstock down over the box. Turn it over and press down firmly until set.

8 Draw another rectangle of stiff cardstock 7⅞ in x 9⅞ in (20 cm x 25 cm). Cut it out and glue it to the underside of the base to make it stronger.

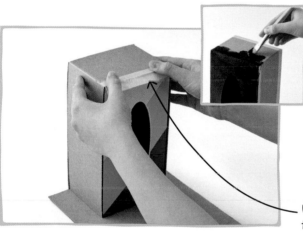

Most launchpads have a tower to hold the rocket upright before take-off.

Use masking tape so you can paint over it.

9 Run a strip of masking tape over all joints, then paint the whole base with black paint and leave to dry. You might need two coats of paint.

10 To make the "steel framework," use silver washi tape. Tape four parallel stripes around the box, tucking the ends into the opening.

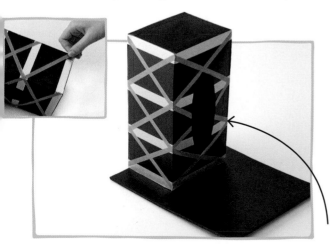

To find the center, draw diagonal lines from opposite corners; they will intersect in the center.

Use thinner silver tape for the crossbars if you have it.

11 Next, add criss-cross diagonal strips of silver washi tape between the horizontal stripes to make the crossbars.

12 In the center of the top of the box, draw a circle the same diameter as the tubing. Make a hole with a pencil, then cut out the circle.

PREPARE FOR LIFT-OFF!

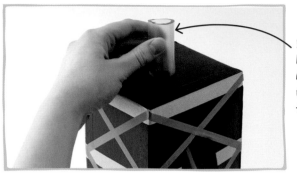

Later, once you've launched your rocket, blow into the tube to reinflate the bottle for the next launch.

1 Push one end of the tubing through the oval opening in the launcher and then through the hole in the top so that a bit sticks up.

2 Attach the other end of the tubing securely to the plastic bottle with duct tape. Make sure the seal is completely airtight.

3 Carefully insert the top section of tubing up into the body of your rocket, then lower the rocket so it's standing on the launcher.

A blast of air launches the rocket into the sky.

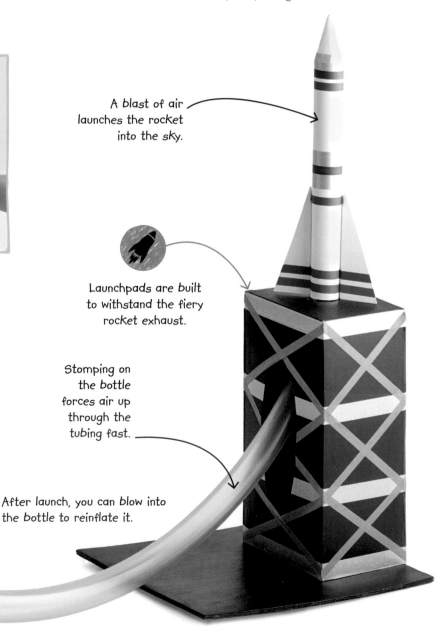

Launchpads are built to withstand the fiery rocket exhaust.

4 Take your launcher outside, start the countdown, then stomp on the plastic bottle. We have lift-off! Reinflate the bottle, then you're ready to go again ...

Stomping on the bottle forces air up through the tubing fast.

After launch, you can blow into the bottle to reinflate it.

HOW IT WORKS

Stomping on the bottle forces air into your rocket. Trapped by its sealed top, the air pushes against it, creating a force that lifts the whole rocket upward, called thrust. A real rocket uses an engine to produce expanding gas but creates thrust in the same way—gas pushes up against the top of the engine but can escape through the exhaust at the bottom, so there is an overall upward force on the rocket.

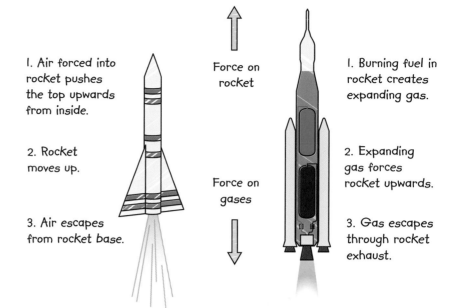

1. Air forced into rocket pushes the top upwards from inside.

2. Rocket moves up.

3. Air escapes from rocket base.

Force on rocket

Force on gases

1. Burning fuel in rocket creates expanding gas.

2. Expanding gas forces rocket upwards.

3. Gas escapes through rocket exhaust.

Rocket model

Real rocket

SPACE SCIENCE
HOW ROCKETS REACH SPACE

In order to avoid falling back to Earth, rockets must create an upward thrust force strong enough to overcome the downward pull of their own weight. The best way to do this is with solid or liquid chemicals called propellants, which burn together in an explosive reaction that pushes hot gases out of exhaust nozzles at the base of the rocket.

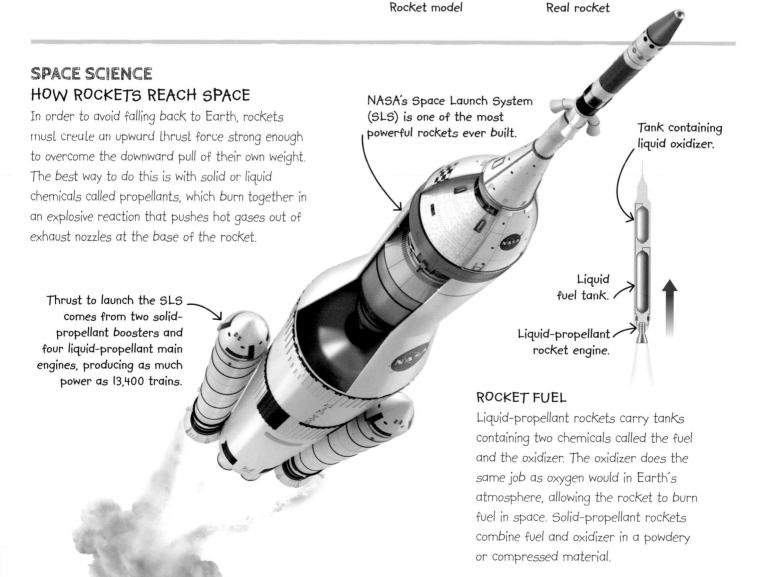

NASA's Space Launch System (SLS) is one of the most powerful rockets ever built.

Tank containing liquid oxidizer.

Liquid fuel tank.

Liquid-propellant rocket engine.

Thrust to launch the SLS comes from two solid-propellant boosters and four liquid-propellant main engines, producing as much power as 13,400 trains.

ROCKET FUEL

Liquid-propellant rockets carry tanks containing two chemicals called the fuel and the oxidizer. The oxidizer does the same job as oxygen would in Earth's atmosphere, allowing the rocket to burn fuel in space. Solid-propellant rockets combine fuel and oxidizer in a powdery or compressed material.

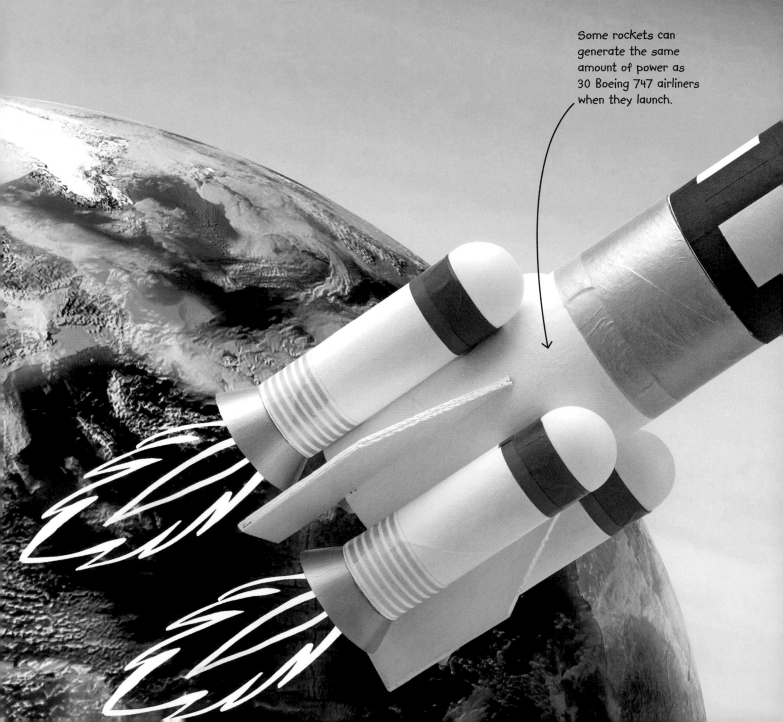

PREPARE TO LAUNCH!
ROCKET MODEL

Rockets are the launch vehicles for getting a spacecraft into space. After that, the rocket sections detach from the spacecraft and fall away. Just like a real rocket, your model is cleverly designed to slot together in four sections.

Some rockets can generate the same amount of power as 30 Boeing 747 airliners when they launch.

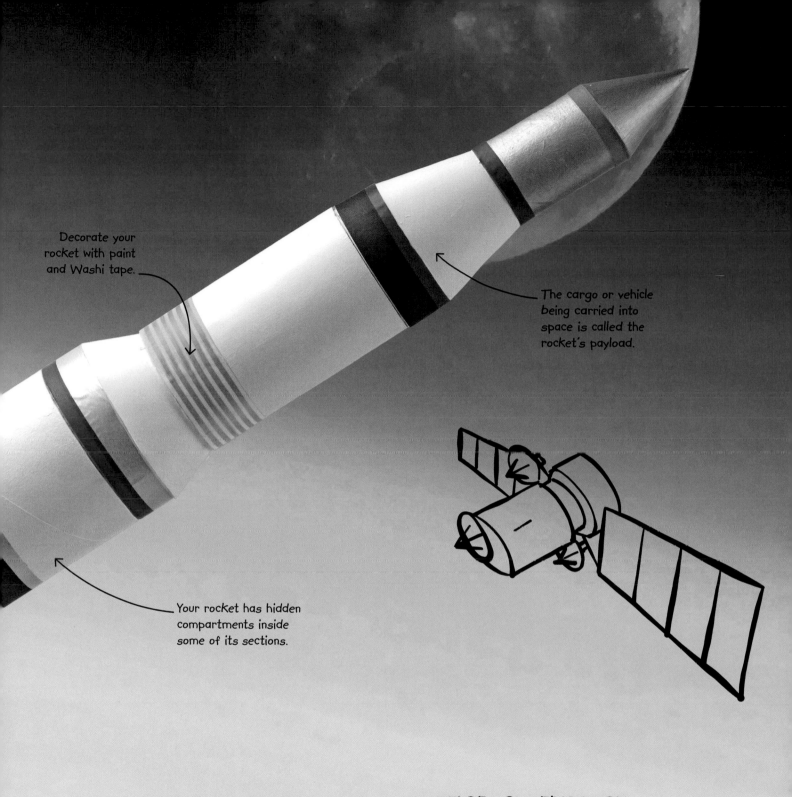

Decorate your rocket with paint and Washi tape.

The cargo or vehicle being carried into space is called the rocket's payload.

Your rocket has hidden compartments inside some of its sections.

STAGES OF SEPARATION

Most rockets are divided into sections called stages, stacked on top of each other, with booster rockets strapped onto the sides. Each stage fires its own powerful rocket engines in succession, then, once its fuel is exhausted, it falls away so that only the lighter upper stages carry on toward space.

MAKE YOUR OWN
SPACE ROCKET

Basically lots of cones and cylinders slotted together, this rocket build is split into sections to make it easy to follow. We've suggested decoration ideas, but it's your rocket, so it's up to you ...

Time
2 hours

Difficulty
Medium

WHAT YOU NEED

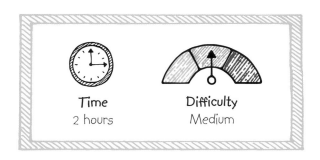

Ruler

Pencil

Paintbrush

Stiff cardstock

Tracing paper

White cardstock

Scissors

Compass

White glue

4 ping-pong balls

Tape measure

Masking tape

Acrylic paints

Large cardboard tube 13 in (33 cm) long, 3³/₁₆ in (8 cm) diameter

Medium cardboard tube 6⁷/₈ in (17.5 cm) long, 2³/₈ in (6 cm) diameter

Washi tape

5 small cardboard tubes 4 in (10 cm) long, 1⁹/₁₆ in (4 cm) diameter

MAKE SECTION 1

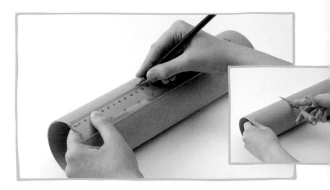

1 Around the large tube, mark off 4³/₄ in (12 cm) from one end. Join the marks into a line, push a pencil into it to make a hole, then insert scissors and cut the tube into a large and a small cylinder.

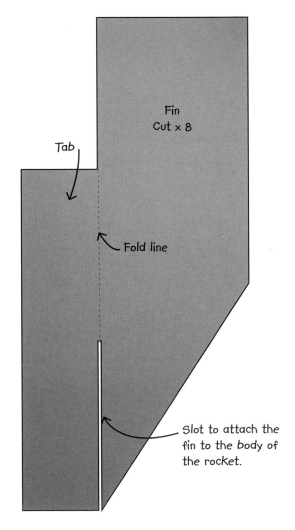

Fin
Cut x 8

Tab

Fold line

Slot to attach the fin to the body of the rocket.

2 Trace the fin shape onto tracing paper and transfer it onto a piece of stiff cardstock. Cut out the fin, including the slot, then cut seven more.

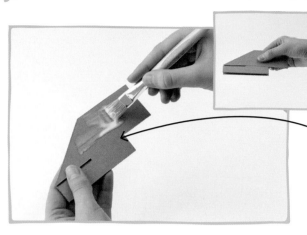

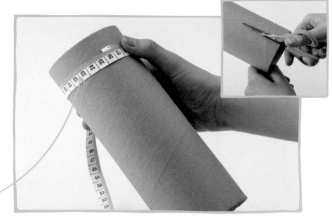

Leave the tabs free of glue, as you'll stick those down later.

Divide the measurement into four equal sections.

3 Glue two fin pieces together, leaving the tab area clear. Repeat for the other six fin pieces to make four double-thickness fins in total.

4 Measure the circumference of the larger cylinder at one end and mark it off into four quarters. At each mark, cut a slot 2 in (5 cm) long.

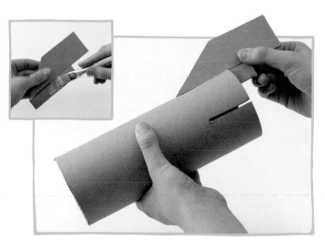

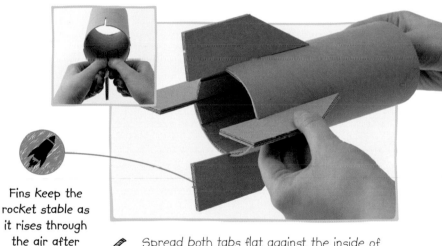

Fins keep the rocket stable as it rises through the air after liftoff.

5 Apply glue to the outer side of each tab on one fin and slide the fin slot into one of the four slots you made in Step 4.

6 Spread both tabs flat against the inside of the cylinder and press firmly until the glue sets. Repeat for the other three fins.

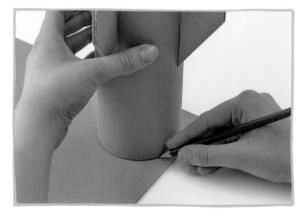

Ease the circle into the cylinder, then push it gently down with a ruler or pencil.

7 Draw around the other end of the cylinder twice onto cardstock. Cut out both circles, staying just within the lines, so they fit inside the cylinder.

8 Push one circle inside the cylinder and slide it down so that it rests on top of the fin tabs glued inside the other end of the cylinder.

MAKE SECTION 2

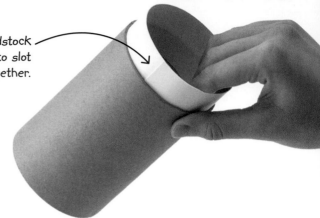

The white cardstock strips will be used to slot the sections together.

Draw a line lengthwise to divide the strip in two, then put glue on one half.

1 Cut a strip of white cardstock 1⁹⁄₁₆ in (4 cm) wide and long enough to fit around the smaller cylinder you made earlier. Apply glue along one half of it.

2 Stick the glued half of the strip inside one end of the cylinder, up to the halfway line, so that the unglued half sticks out of the cylinder.

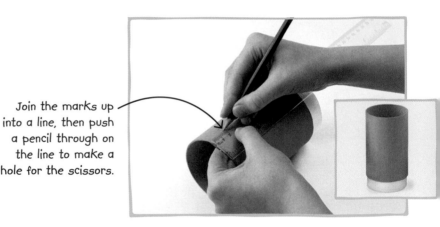

Join the marks up into a line, then push a pencil through on the line to make a hole for the scissors.

3 Push the second circle you made earlier into the other end of the cylinder. Ease it all the way along until it rests against the white strip.

4 At the end with no white strip, mark off a section ¾ in (2 cm) from the end of the cylinder. Cut it off, ready to use for section 3.

MAKE SECTION 3

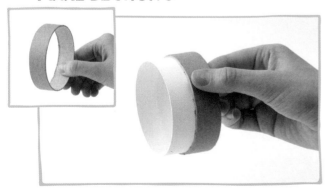

Draw a line through the compass point to divide the circle in two.

1 On the ¾-in (2-cm) section of cylinder you just cut, glue another strip of white cardstock 1⁹⁄₁₆ in (4 cm) wide half-in, half-out, around the inside of it.

2 Use a compass to draw a circle with a radius of 4 in (10 cm) on white cardstock. Cut it out, then cut it in half. Save one semicircle for later.

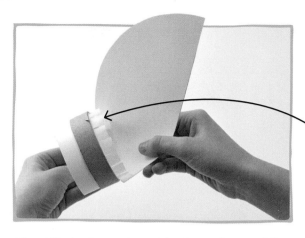

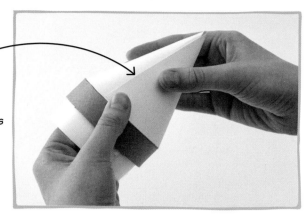

Glue along the straight joint.

Use your fingers and thumb to press the card onto the sticky outside face of the tape pieces.

3 Attach pieces of masking tape all around the inside of the cylinder at the end without the white strip. Start sticking the curved edge of one semicircle to the pieces of tape.

4 Carefully bend the semicircle around, sticking it onto all the pieces of tape to form a cone. Glue the cone together and hold until set.

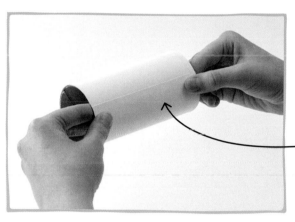

This will give your finished rocket a more polished look.

5 If the medium cardboard tube is rough or has grooves running around it, wrap it with a piece of white cardstock and glue in place.

6 Slot the medium tube over the pointed end of the cone. Sit the tube level and draw a line around it on the cone.

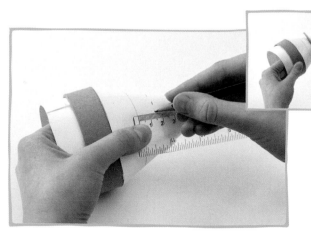

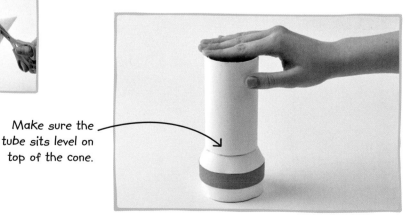

Make sure the tube sits level on top of the cone.

7 About 9⁄16 in (1.5 cm) up from the line you have just drawn, mark off a second line. Cut along it to remove the top of the cone, which you don't need.

8 Apply glue inside one end of the medium tube, then stick it to the remainder of the cone, making sure it sits level. Hold until set.

Outer rocket
casings need to
be lightweight
but strong.

9 On stiff cardstock, draw around the other end of the cylinder. Cut out the circle, and slide it down into the tube until it rests on the cut-off cone.

10 At the end of the cylinder without the cut-off cone, make a series of marks ¾ in (2 cm) from the end, and join them up with a line.

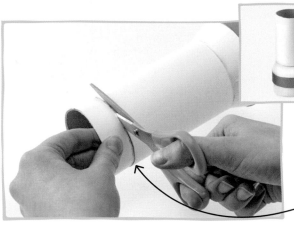

As before, push
a pencil through
the tube first to
make a hole for
your scissors.

11 Cut along the line to take off the ¾-in (2-cm) segment of the cylinder, ready to be used for section 4.

MAKE SECTION 4

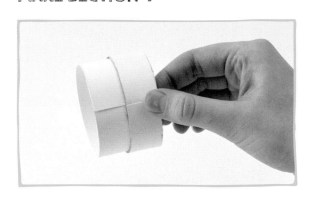

1 Cut another strip of white cardstock 1⁹/₁₆ in (4 cm) wide. Stick it inside the ¾-in (2-cm) segment you just made—half-in, half-out, as before.

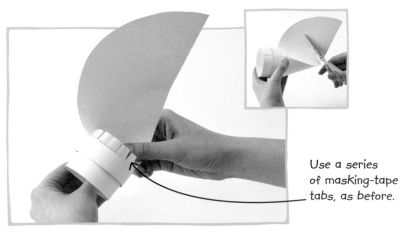

Use a series
of masking-tape
tabs, as before.

2 Use the remaining semicircle to make a cone on the other end (see page 79, Steps 3 and 4). Trim to size, glue it together, and hold until set.

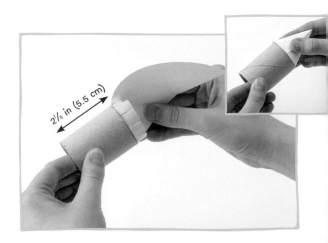

2⅛ in (5.5 cm)

3 Cut a small tube down to 2³/₁₆ in (5.5 cm). On white cardstock, draw and cut out a semi-circle with a 2-in (5-cm) radius, to make a cone at one end.

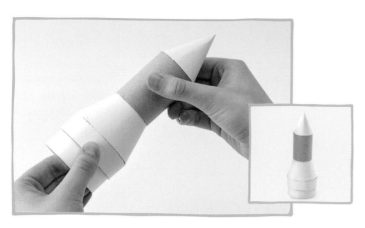

4 Glue the open end of the small tube over the top of the cone you made in Step 2. Hold in place until set, making sure it's sitting level.

5 Give all four sections of your rocket a coat of white paint, adding a second coat of paint as necessary. Leave to dry.

MAKE THE BOOSTERS

Boosters provide extra thrust for launch and are jettisoned over the ocean after use.

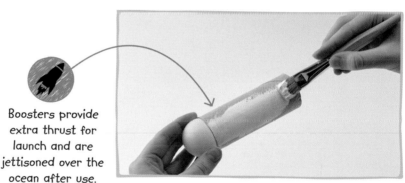

6 Once dry, paint the insides of sections 1, 2, and 3 black, but don't worry about painting the inside of section 4.

1 Glue a ping-pong ball into one end of each of the four remaining small tubes. Hold until set, then paint the tubes white. (You may need two coats.)

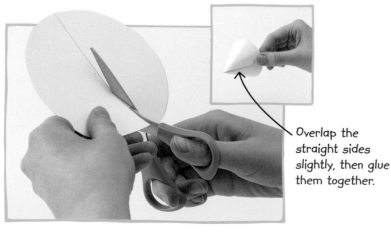

Overlap the straight sides slightly, then glue them together.

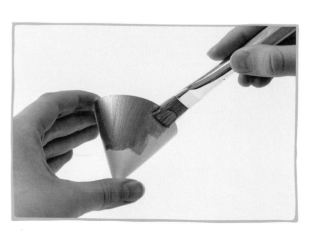

2 Cut two circles with a 2⅜-in (6-cm) radius out of white cardstock, then cut them in half. Glue each semicircle into a cone shape, holding until set.

3 Paint the four cones silver. You might need a couple of coats of paint to make sure they are completely covered. Leave to dry.

4 Apply glue to the inside of the open end of each tube. Insert a silver cone into each one, and hold in place until the glue sets.

5 Decorate your *boosters* with Washi tape, making sure the two ends of the tape join up level around the tubes.

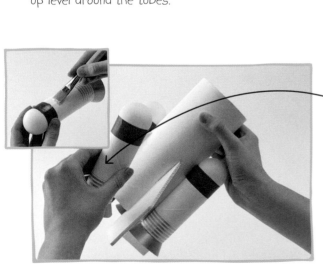

6 Paint a stripe of glue along each of the four boosters and stick them onto Section 1, in between the fins.

Paint the top of your rocket silver.

Keep the cone base parallel with the end of the tube.

The nose cone contains a crew escape module for use in an emergency.

SECTION 4

Add stripes of Washi-tape decoration.

SECTION 3

The cylinders slot over the white card strips, which hold them together.

SECTION 2

The boosters help the main engine generate the massive power needed for launch.

Make sure you glue the boosters level with each other.

SECTION 1

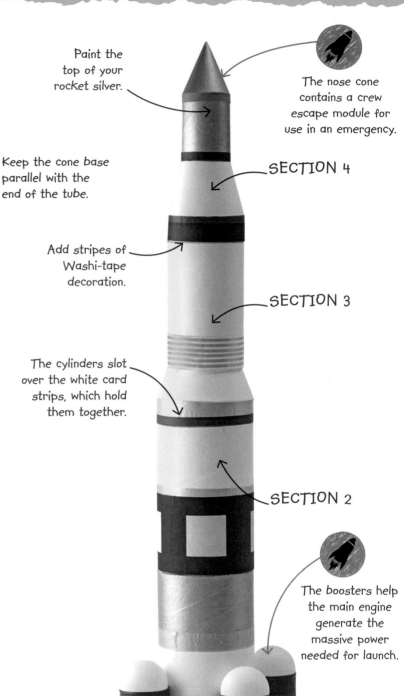

7 Finally, slot the four rocket sections together and finish decorating it. Follow our suggestions, copy your favorite rocket, or make up your own design.

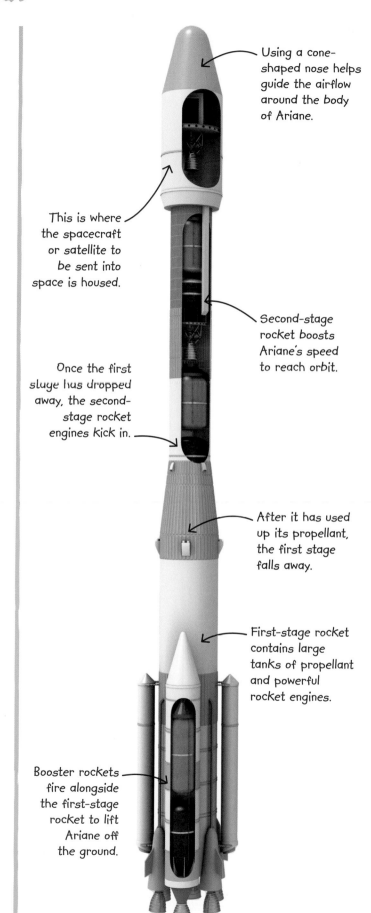

Using a cone-shaped nose helps guide the airflow around the body of Ariane.

This is where the spacecraft or satellite to be sent into space is housed.

Once the first stage has dropped away, the second-stage rocket engines kick in.

Second-stage rocket boosts Ariane's speed to reach orbit.

After it has used up its propellant, the first stage falls away.

First-stage rocket contains large tanks of propellant and powerful rocket engines.

Booster rockets fire alongside the first-stage rocket to lift Ariane off the ground.

SPACE SCIENCE
ROCKET DESIGNS
Your model is based on one of the most common rocket designs used today, for instance by this European Space Agency Ariane (see left). But the size and number of stages in a rocket system can vary depending on how heavy the payload (cargo being delivered into space) is and how fast it needs to be launched. Reusable rockets such as SpaceX's Falcon 9 have lower stages that can make a guided return to Earth, ready to be launched again.

ROCKET SECRETS
Thanks to the way your model is constructed, it actually creates hidden compartments, which you could use to stow things you want to keep out of sight or even just to organize your desk. Sections 1, 2, and 3 all have secret compartments built into them that are only revealed once the different sections are taken apart.

Store markers and crayons in your rocket's secret compartments to keep your desk neat and tidy.

This helmet is papier mâché, but real astronaut helmets are made of a very strong material called high-impact polycarbonate plastic.

Make your visor from clear plastic; real visors have filters to protect astronauts' eyes.

Make your helmet loose-fitting so that air can flow freely in and out.

VISORS DOWN!
SPACE HELMET

Without a spacesuit to provide oxygen and pressure, no astronaut would survive in space, and a helmet is an essential part of any astronaut's equipment. Get ready for your space mission with this papier-mâché helmet as part of your space kit.

WHY ASTRONAUTS WEAR HELMETS

A helmet is a very important part of any spacesuit. It creates an environment in which an astronaut can breathe, protects their head, keeps them in touch with their base via a radio link, and acts as a window to see out of.

MAKE YOUR OWN
ASTRONAUT HELMET

Your helmet needs to fit over your head, and you must be able to breathe easily, so test for fit and make it loose enough for air to flow. For the visor, you can use acetate or any stiff plastic packaging otherwise destined for the recycling bin.

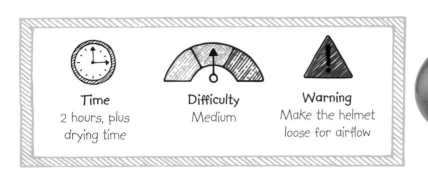

Time
2 hours, plus drying time

Difficulty
Medium

Warning
Make the helmet loose for airflow

WHAT YOU NEED

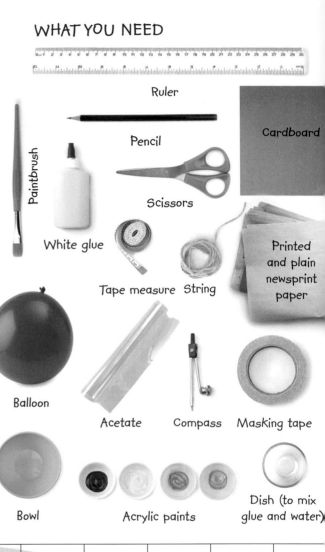

Ruler

Pencil

Cardboard

Paintbrush

White glue

Scissors

Tape measure   String

Printed and plain newsprint paper

Balloon

Acetate   Compass   Masking tape

Bowl   Acrylic paints   Dish (to mix glue and water)

VISOR TEMPLATE

To copy and enlarge this template, draw a grid of squares on your cardstock. Then just copy the shapes in each square on this grid across into the larger squares on your card.

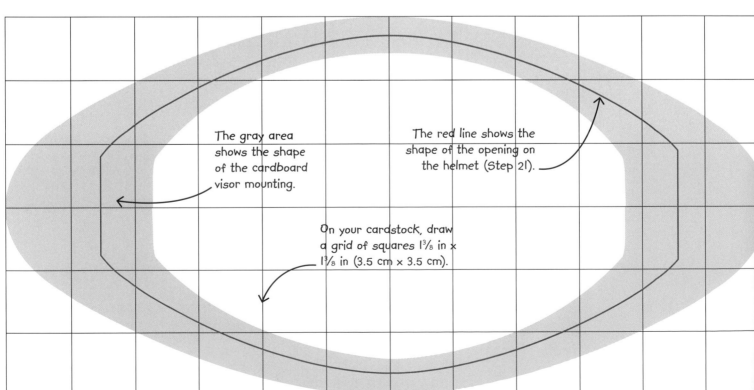

The gray area shows the shape of the cardboard visor mounting.

The red line shows the shape of the opening on the helmet (Step 21).

On your cardstock, draw a grid of squares 1⅜ in x 1⅜ in (3.5 cm x 3.5 cm).

The circumference is the distance all around the outside of a circle or sphere.

1 Tear the printed newspaper into about 1½ in (4 cm) squares. You want torn, rough edges, as they will blend together well for the papier mâché.

2 Measure the widest part of your head (and hair). Blow up a round *balloon* to a circumference at least 8 in (20 cm) larger than your head's.

Sit the balloon in a bowl so that it is stable as you work.

3 In a bowl, mix equal amounts of glue and water. Working on one section of balloon at a time, cover it with a layer of overlapping newspaper squares and glue.

4 Glue squares almost up to the neck of the balloon, so that it is nearly covered in a layer of newspaper and glue. Leave the neck area, as it will be cut away later.

Using plain paper helps you see which areas you have already done and which ones you haven't.

5 Repeat Step 1, but this time tearing up the plain newspaper into squares. Remember, you want rough edges, not straight ones.

6 Using the plain squares, repeat Steps 3–4. As before, overlap the edges and go almost up to the neck of the balloon.

Tie the string around the neck of the balloon.

7 Hang the balloon up overnight to let the papier mâché dry fully. Make sure the balloon hangs free and doesn't touch anything.

8 Once it has dried, repeat Steps 3–7 so the balloon has four layers of newspaper in total—printed, plain, printed, plain.

Space helmets are white to reflect sunlight and keep the temperature as even as possible.

9 Paint the papier mâché white and leave to dry. If you can still see newsprint through the paint, repeat to make the helmet completely white.

10 After the paint has dried, pop the balloon. Cut a little hole by the knot and carefully pull the balloon out from inside the papier mâché.

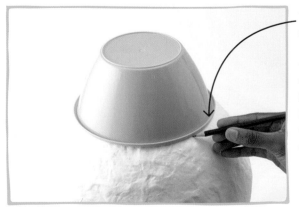

The circumference must be at least 1½ in (4 cm) larger than that of the widest part of your head (including hair)—air must be able to flow in and out of the helmet.

11 Place a bowl over the open end of the helmet and draw around it. This is to make the opening through which your head will fit.

12 Carefully cut around the pencil line to form a neat hole. If you find it easier, cut away the papier mâché in pieces.

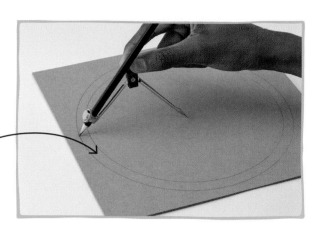

The gap between the two circles will be ⁹/₁₆ in (1.5 cm).

13 Check that the helmet fits easily over your head. Mark off and cut away a bit more papier mâché if necessary to get a loose fit.

14 Measure across the opening of the helmet. Draw one circle with that diameter and a second circle with a diameter 1³/₁₆ in (3 cm) bigger.

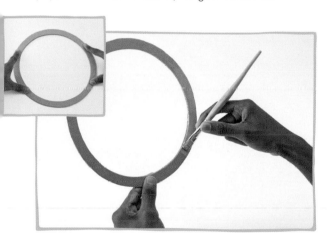

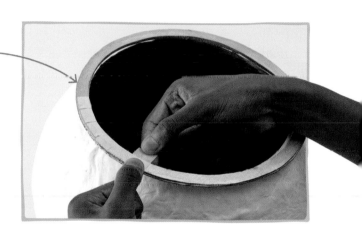

Helmets lock onto a spacesuit collar, making a seal that keeps air inside.

15 Repeat Step 14 to draw another two circles on cardstock. Cut out the larger circles, then the inner ones. Glue the two rings together and cover in silver paint. Leave to dry.

16 Secure the ring to the opening of the helmet with strips of masking tape. Line them up with the outer edge of the ring and fold around inside the helmet.

17 Next, paint the inside of the helmet black and let it dry. You may need two coats of paint to make the inside totally black.

Paint over the masking tape inside the helmet, too.

18 Paint the side of the ring facing out in black, to cover the masking tape, then leave to dry.

Copy the gray area on the template, one square at a time.

Draw a grid of squares, with each line 1³⁄₈ in (3.5 cm) apart.

19 On a piece of stiff cardstock 16½ in x 8¼ in (42 cm x 21 cm), draw a grid to copy and enlarge the gray visor mounting shape on page 86.

20 Once you have copied the gray visor mounting shape, cut it out. Paint it silver on both sides and leave to dry.

Push a pencil gently through first to make a hole for the scissors.

21 Lay the visor on the helmet. Draw around the inside of it to help you copy the opening shape (the red line on the template). Cut out the opening.

22 Apply glue to one side of the visor mounting and carefully lay a piece of acetate flat over it, then press the acetate onto the glue.

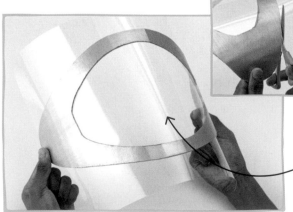

Any stiff, flexible plastic will work, such as cellophane packaging.

The visor is glued only at either end, to leave plenty of room for air flow.

23 While the glue is setting, bend the visor so it sets in position. Once it has set, carefully cut away the excess acetate.

24 Apply glue to each end of the visor and stick them in place on either side of the helmet, loosely covering the opening.

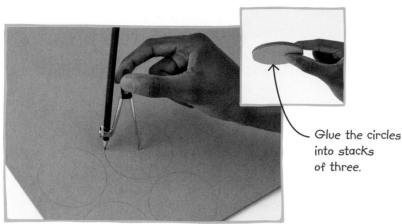

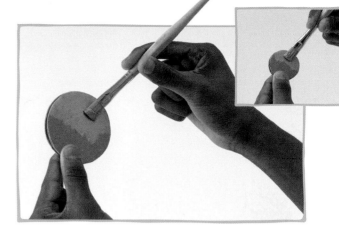

Glue the circles into stacks of three.

25 Make six cardstock circles with a radius of 1⅜ in (3.5 cm) and six with a ¾-in (2-cm) radius. Glue the large circles in two stacks of three, then repeat for the small circles.

26 Paint the two large stacks silver and the two small stacks gold and leave to dry. Add a second coat of paint if necessary.

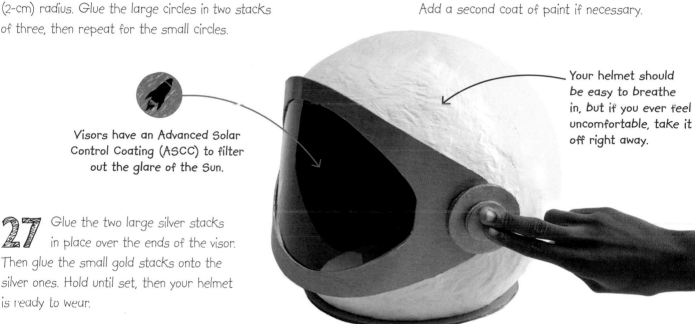

Visors have an Advanced Solar Control Coating (ASCC) to filter out the glare of the Sun.

Your helmet should be easy to breathe in, but if you ever feel uncomfortable, take it off right away.

27 Glue the two large silver stacks in place over the ends of the visor. Then glue the small gold stacks onto the silver ones. Hold until set, then your helmet is ready to wear.

SPACE SCIENCE
HELMET DESIGN

Early astronaut helmets had small glass windows on the front, but modern helmets are made of stronger materials and can have bubble-shaped visors. This allows astronauts to look around more easily, with a wider field of vision.

Italian astronaut Samantha Cristoforetti looks out of her space helmet during underwater training.

OXYGEN TANKS

With no air in space, how do astronauts breathe? Well, for any mission outside the spaceship, they strap on a portable life-support system (PLSS). Make this project to go with your space helmet and you'll soon be ready for your spacewalk!

WHAT IS A PLSS?

This essential part of an astronaut's spacesuit supplies oxygen and extracts the carbon-dioxide waste breathed out. It also helps keep the astronaut cool and provides battery power and radio communications.

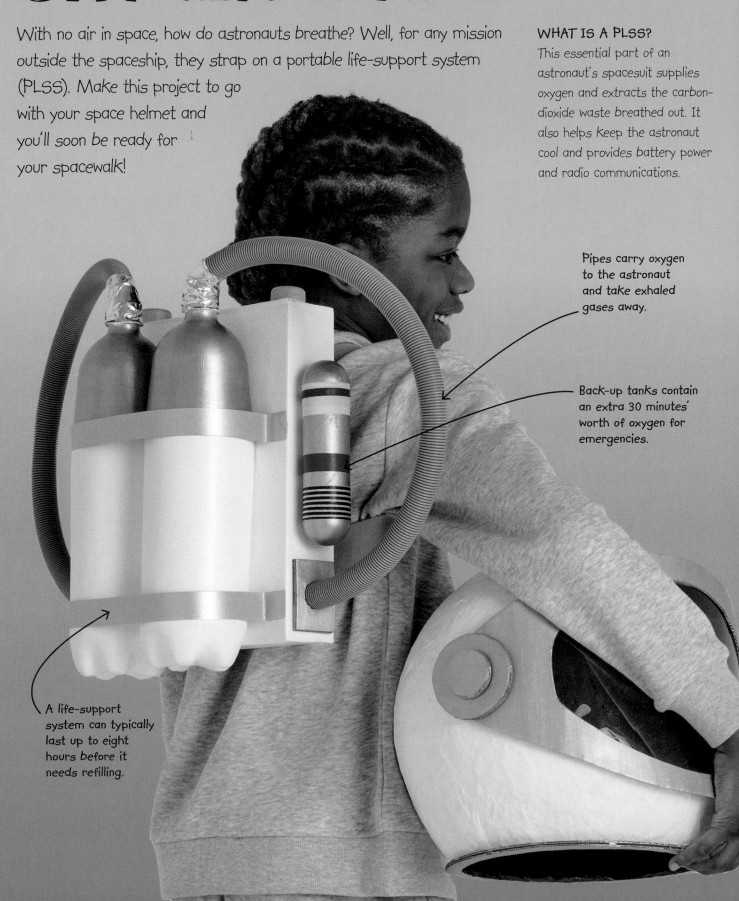

Pipes carry oxygen to the astronaut and take exhaled gases away.

Back-up tanks contain an extra 30 minutes' worth of oxygen for emergencies.

A life-support system can typically last up to eight hours before it needs refilling.

MAKE YOUR OWN
OXYGEN TANKS

Raid the recycling bin for this project; it uses empty soda bottles for the tanks and old tubing or hose for the piping. You wear it like a backpack, so make sure the elastic strips are long enough to fit you.

Time
2 hours, plus drying time

Difficulty
Medium

WHAT YOU NEED

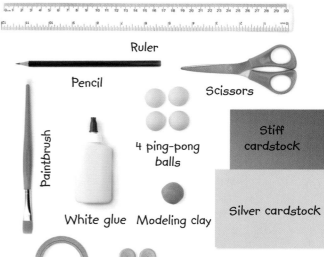

Ruler

Pencil

Scissors

4 ping-pong balls

Stiff cardstock

Paintbrush

White glue   Modeling clay

Silver cardstock

Silver duct tape

Bottle tops

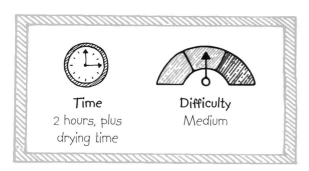

2 empty 2-liter plastic soda bottles

Stapler

2 pieces of plastic tubing 23½ in (60 cm) long

2 small cardboard tubes   Compass

2 strips of wide gray elastic, about 22 in (55 cm) long

Washi tape

Acrylic paints

BACKPACK TEMPLATE

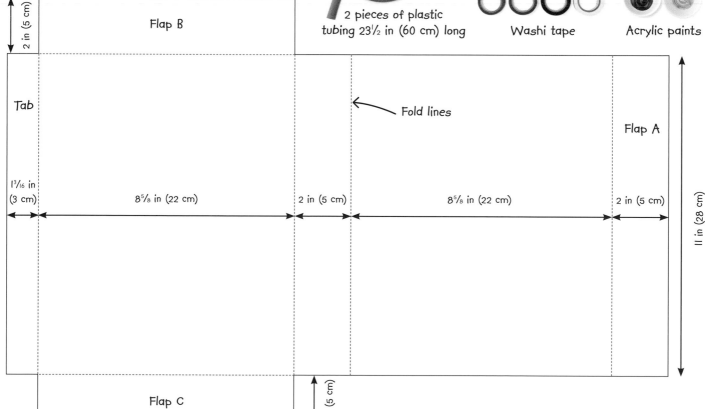

Flap B

Tab

Fold lines

Flap A

2 in (5 cm)

1³/₁₆ in (3 cm)

8⅝ in (22 cm)

2 in (5 cm)

8⅝ in (22 cm)

2 in (5 cm)

11 in (28 cm)

Flap C

2 in (5 cm)

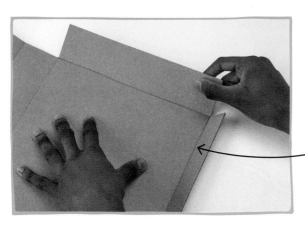

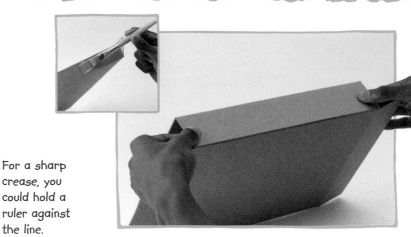

For a sharp crease, you could hold a ruler against the line.

1 To make the backpack, copy the template onto stiff cardstock. Cut it out, crease along all the fold lines, and bend them inward.

2 Apply glue to the back of the tab. Fold the cardstock around to stick Flap A onto the glued side of the tab. Press firmly until set.

A reflective white coating stops the PLSS from overheating in fierce sunlight.

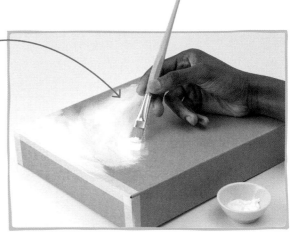

3 Fold over Flaps B and C and tape them in place with masking tape to complete your box shape.

4 Paint the box white and leave it to dry. You may need two coats of paint to make sure it's completely white.

The PLSS always carries two tanks so astronauts have plenty of oxygen.

Keep the bottle tops—you'll need them in Step 30.

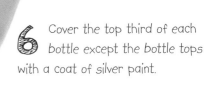

5 For the two main oxygen tanks, paint the two plastic bottles with white paint and leave to dry. Again, you may need two coats of paint.

6 Cover the top third of each bottle except the bottle tops with a coat of silver paint.

Don't worry if this line is a little wonky—it will be covered up later.

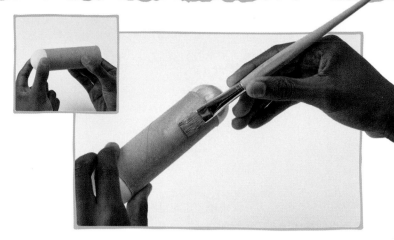

7 Let the paint dry. Add a second coat if necessary.

8 To make the back-up tanks, glue a ping-pong ball to either end of both cardboard tubes. Let the glue set, then paint them both silver.

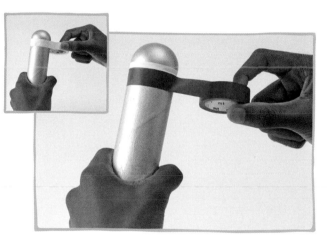

Keep your stripes perpendicular to the tube so they line up.

9 Begin adding stripes of Washi tape to a tube. Layer one strip of tape over another if you want to have some thinner stripes.

10 Roll the tape carefully around the tube to make sure that your stripes meet up with each other.

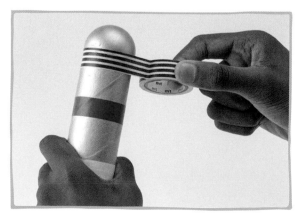

11 Add as many different colors or effects as you want. If you don't have Washi tape, you could color some masking tape instead.

12 Once you've decorated the first tube, copy the pattern onto the second tube so you have two matching back-up tanks.

13 Cut two rectangles of cardstock 7 in × 9½ in (18 cm × 24 cm). Within one rectangle, draw a second rectangle ¾ in (2 cm) smaller on all sides.

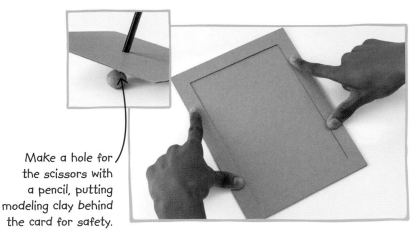

Make a hole for the scissors with a pencil, putting modeling clay behind the card for safety.

14 Cut out the smaller rectangle to leave a "frame." Glue it to the full rectangle, lining up the outer edges of both.

15 Lay an elastic strip inside the frame. Mark off the width of it at either end. Repeat for the other strip along the other side of the frame.

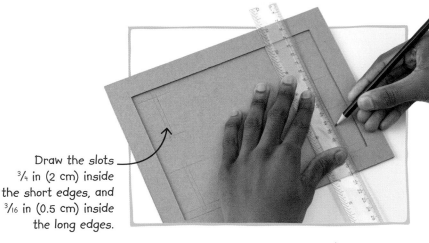

Draw the slots ¾ in (2 cm) inside the short edges, and ³⁄₁₆ in (0.5 cm) inside the long edges.

16 In each of the four corners, draw a horizontal slot slightly wider than the strips and about ³⁄₁₆ in (0.5 cm) deep.

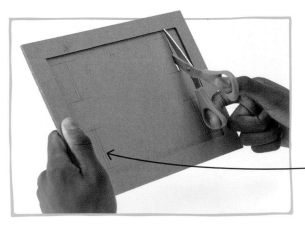

These slots will hold the backpack-style straps.

17 Make a hole with a pencil (see Step 14) in each of the four slots you've drawn, then insert your scissors and carefully cut out the slots.

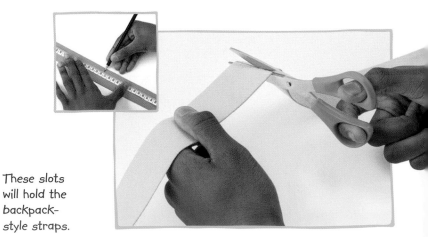

18 Measure the two elastic strips to make sure they're long enough to fit you. Cut to length, allowing 1 in (2.5 cm) extra for overlap, too.

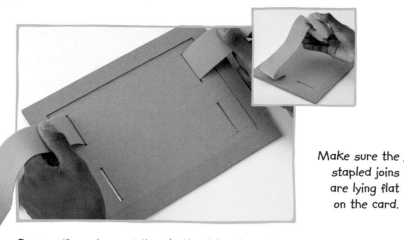

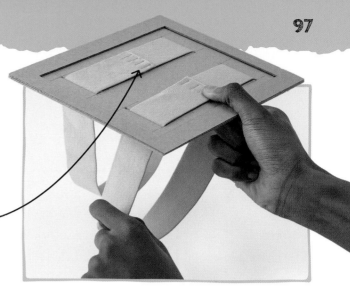

Make sure the stapled joins are lying flat on the card.

19 Thread one of the elastic strips through two slots, as shown. Overlap the two ends of the elastic by 1 in (2.5 cm) and staple together.

20 Repeat Step 19 for the second strip of elastic, then pull both loops through so that the stapled joins sit flush inside the frame.

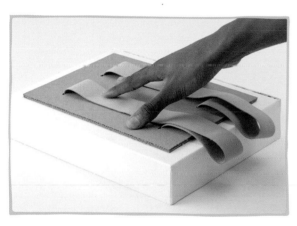

Where the two diagonal lines intersect is the center of the shape.

21 Glue the frame onto one side of the white box. Press firmly until set.

22 For the tubing connectors, cut six cardstock rectangles 2³⁄₈ in × 1⁹⁄₁₆ in (6 cm × 4 cm). To find the centers, draw lines from corner to corner.

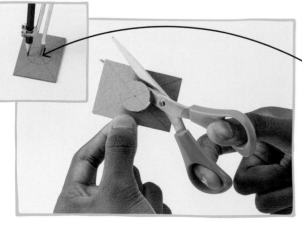

Put your compass in the center, where the lines intersect.

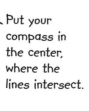

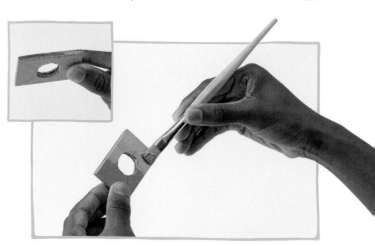

23 Measure the diameter of the tubing. Use a compass to draw a central circle of the same size on each rectangle. Cut out each circle.

24 Glue the rectangles into two stacks of three, holding until set. Paint them silver and leave to dry. Add a second coat if necessary.

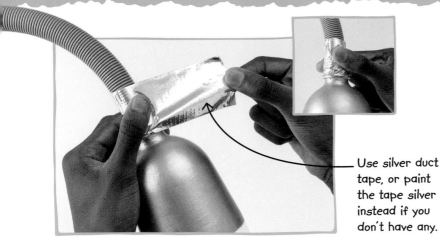

Use silver duct tape, or paint the tape silver instead if you don't have any.

25 Unscrew the bottle tops. (Keep them for Step 30.) Tape one end of the tubing to a bottle neck. Repeat for the other bottle and tubing.

26 Glue the two bottles side by side, neck toward you, onto the white side of the box. Hold until the glue sets.

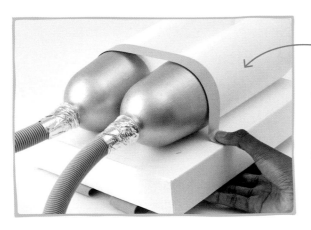

A bulky backpack helps shield an astronaut's body from dangerous radiation in space.

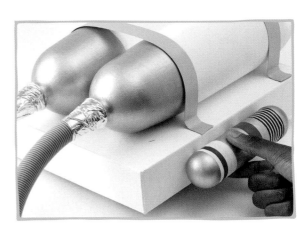

27 Cut two long strips of silver cardstock 1 in (2.5 cm) wide. Glue them in place at the top and bottom of the bottles and trim off any excess.

28 Next, glue the back-up tanks on either side of the box, making sure they line up with each other. Hold until set.

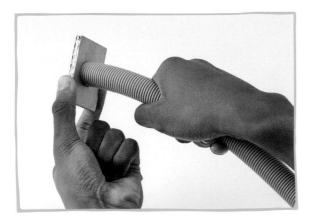

Position the connectors below the back-up tanks.

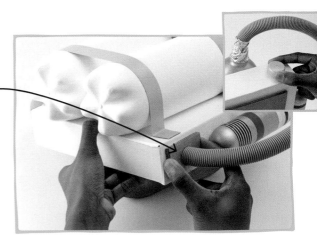

29 Insert the loose ends of the tubing into the tubing connectors you made in Steps 22–24. Glue them in position.

30 Glue a tubing connector to either side of the box, lining them up with each other. Finally, glue the bottle tops onto the top of the box.

The bottle tops make great control knobs for your life-support system.

A PLSS contains a radio for talking to other astronauts and the team back on Earth.

A backpack sometimes has a hard outer casing to protect it from damage.

31 Once the glue has set, the PLSS is ready to strap on and you're equipped for your first spacewalk.

SPACE SCIENCE
SURVIVING IN SPACE

A life-support system is just one part of the spacesuit that allows an astronaut to work outside a spaceship. Once the helmet is in place and the suit is sealed, the PLSS manages the astronaut's air supply. The suit itself takes an hour to put on and is designed to protect an astronaut and control their body temperature as they move from scorching sunlight to freezing shade.

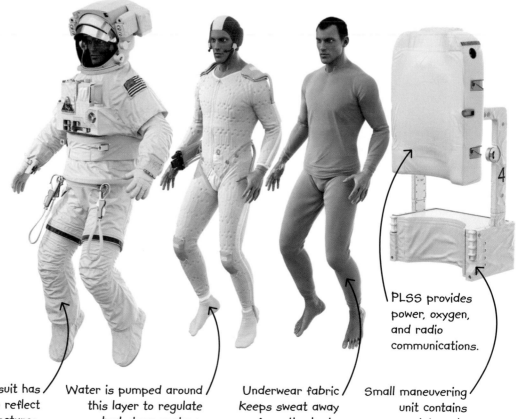

The outer spacesuit has 14 different layers to reflect heat and resist punctures.

Water is pumped around this layer to regulate body temperature.

Underwear fabric keeps sweat away from the body.

Small maneuvering unit contains a jet pack.

PLSS provides power, oxygen, and radio communications.

LUNAR ROVER

Wheeled rovers help us learn about other worlds. This project is based on the sort of rover future astronauts might use for long journeys of lunar exploration. Real rovers are powered by batteries and solar power, but this one will be powered by you—and two rubber bands!

Headlamps on a real rover are for lighting up dangerous shadows.

ROVERS IN SPACE
Several robotic rovers have explored the surface of the Moon and Mars, sending information back to Earth. Astronauts also took short drives on the Moon in 1971, using a rover a bit like a very large go-kart. Future exploratory journeys may be done in rovers more like this one, with pressurized cabins for astronauts so they don't have to wear spacesuits.

Add as many instruments and panels as you want onto your rover.

Observation dome for viewing the surface.

MAKE YOUR OWN
MOON BUGGY

This buggy is powered by rubber band. Pull the buggy backward to stretch the band, then release it and the energy stored in the band will drive the buggy forward.

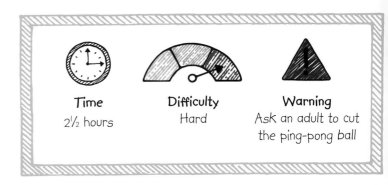

Time
2½ hours

Difficulty
Hard

Warning
Ask an adult to cut the ping-pong ball

TEMPLATES

To copy and enlarge these shapes, draw a grid of squares onto cardstock, then copy the shapes in each square into the squares you've drawn.

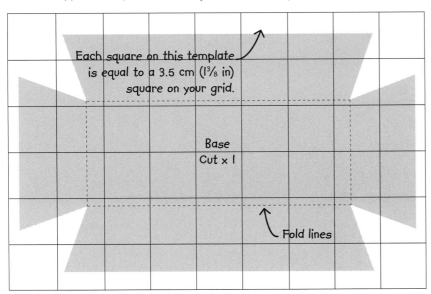

Each square on this template is equal to a 3.5 cm (1⅜ in) square on your grid.

Base
Cut x 1

Fold lines

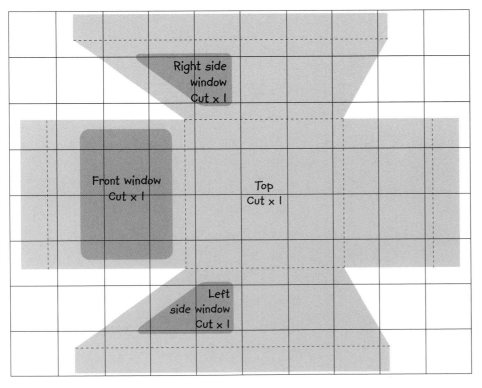

Right side window
Cut x 1

Front window
Cut x 1

Top
Cut x 1

Left side window
Cut x 1

WHAT YOU NEED

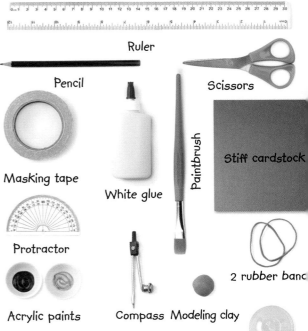

Ruler

Pencil

Scissors

Masking tape

White glue

Paintbrush

Stiff cardstock

Protractor

Acrylic paints

Compass　Modeling clay

2 rubber band

Plastic cup cov

2 dowels 7½ in (19 cm) long

OPTIONAL EXTRAS

4 dowels 4⅜ in (11 cm) long

Dowel 2⅜ in (6 cm) long

Dowel 4 in (10 cm) long

2 thumb tack

Cocktail umbrella

Silver washi tape

Ping-pong ba cut in half

Toothpicks

Colored stickers

Yellow or gold cardstock

MAKE THE BASE

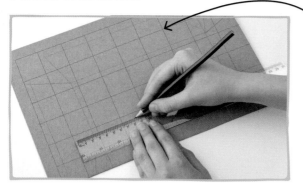

Copying the template shape into your bigger squares will enlarge it.

1 On a piece of cardstock, draw a grid of squares 1³⁄₈ in x 1³⁄₈ in (3.5 cm x 3.5 cm). Use the grid to help you copy the shape of the Base onto the cardstock.

Squaring off the edges will give you corner rules to easily measure from.

2 Cut out the outline. Draw a line along each fold line from edge to edge to make a square at each corner, then cut out the template corners.

3 Fold in the sides to check that the edges come together well. (You could hold a ruler on the lines for sharp creases.)

Make two holes on each of the long sides of the base.

4 On each long side, mark a point ³⁄₄ in (2 cm) from either edge and 1³⁄₁₆ in (3 cm) from the corner rule. Push a hole through the four marks.

Use a ruler to find the middle of a short side.

5 On one short side, ³⁄₁₆ in (0.5 cm) either side of the midpoint, draw a line 1 in (2.5 cm) long straight up from the edge. Cut slits on the two lines.

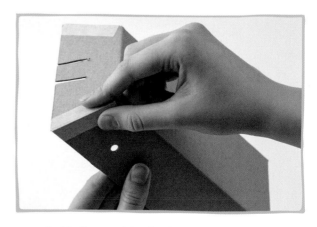

6 Fold all four sides back together again, as for Step 3, but this time secure all the joints with masking tape.

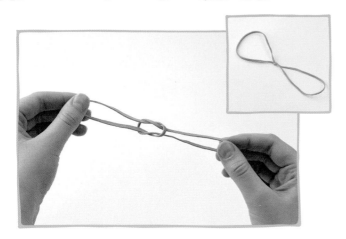

7 Loop two strong rubber bands inside each other, then pull the outer ends tight to knot the rubber bands securely together.

8 Slide one of the loops into the two slits, then pull the rubber band to sit flat against the outside of the base.

This strip will reinforce your buggy and hold the rubber band in place.

9 Cut a small rectangle of cardstock ¾ in × 2⅜ in (2 cm × 6 cm). Glue it over the slits, above the rubber band, on the inside. Hold it in place until the glue sets.

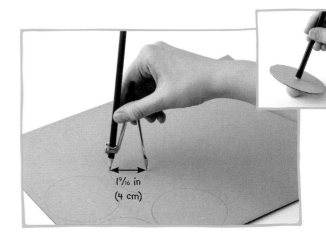

1⁹⁄₁₆ in (4 cm)

10 For the wheels, draw and cut out 24 circles with a 1⁹⁄₁₆ in (4 cm) radius. With modeling clay behind the cardstock for safety, make a hole in the center of each circle with a pencil.

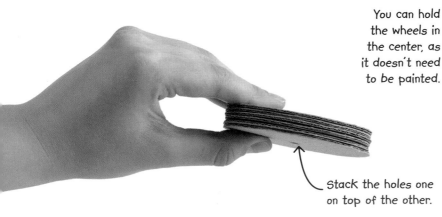

Stack the holes one on top of the other.

11 Lining up all the center holes, glue six circles together for the first wheel. Repeat to make three more wheels with the remaining 18 circles.

You can hold the wheels in the center, as it doesn't need to be painted.

12 Paint the wheels black, including the edges. Don't worry about the areas near the holes, as they'll be covered by hubcaps. Leave to dry.

Remember to put clay behind the card when you pierce the hole.

13 For the hubcaps, make four circles with a ³/₄ in (2 cm) radius and four with a ³/₈ in (1 cm) radius. Punch holes, as before.

14 Glue each small circle onto each large circle, lining up the holes. Let the glue set, then paint them silver.

In engineering, this is called an axle—a simple rod that connects two wheels.

15 Push a dowel into one of the wheels, with ³/₈ in (1 cm) of it sticking through the wheel. Glue it in place, then repeat to glue a wheel to the other dowel.

16 Draw and cut out four circles with a ³/₈ in (1 cm) radius. Make a center hole in each one, as before. These are stoppers for the wheels.

18 Glue on another wheel, as for Step 15. Adjust the stoppers to sit near the two sides to keep the wheels in place.

17 Push the dowel through the hole on one side of the base at the rubber-band end. Slide on two stoppers, then push it through the other side.

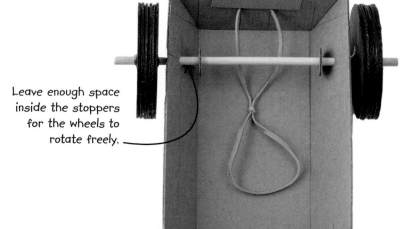

Leave enough space inside the stoppers for the wheels to rotate freely.

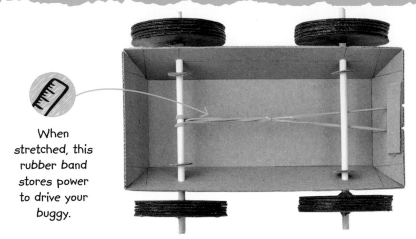

When stretched, this rubber band stores power to drive your buggy.

19 Insert the second dowel into the other end of the base and slide a stopper onto it. Fold the rubber band into a loop, thread the dowel through it, and add a final stopper.

20 Slide the dowel through the other side of the base and glue on the final wheel. Adjust the stoppers and glue them all in place.

MAKE THE TOP

Draw a grid of squares that are 1⅜ in x 1⅜ in (3.5 cm x 3.5 cm).

Where the two diagonal lines intersect marks the center point.

21 Finally, slide the four hubcaps you made in Steps 13-14 onto the dowel ends and glue them to the wheels. Hold until the glue sets.

1 For the top, use a grid again to copy the Top template onto cardstock. Cut it out. Draw diagonal lines across the central square to find the midpoint.

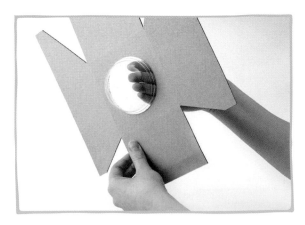

2 Place the plastic cup cover over the central point and draw around it with a pencil. This will be your buggy's observation dome.

3 Cut just inside the line you drew to make a hole slightly smaller than the circle. Push the cup cover up through it and glue in place.

Windows on a buggy have a coating of reflective material to block the Sun's glare.

4 Fold in the sides (you could hold a ruler on the lines for sharp creases) and secure the joints with masking tape.

5 Cover the inside of the top with *black paint* and leave to dry. Add a second coat if you think it needs it.

ASSEMBLE THE BUGGY

1 Slot the top section over the base and stick them together with masking tape. Press to make sure they're firmly attached.

Real buggy wheels have separate motors to cope with rough terrain.

2 Now it's time to add the details. Glue two 4⅜ in (11 cm) dowels to the front and two to the back, over the masking tape, as shown.

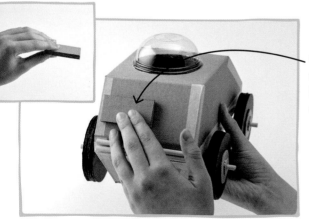

Once painted, this will look like an instrument panel on the buggy.

Ask an adult to cut a ping-pong ball in half.

3 Cut eight rectangles of cardstock ¾ in x 2⅜ in (2 cm x 6 cm). Glue them together in two stacks of four. Stick one on the back and one on the side. Leave to set.

4 Glue one half of a ping-pong ball onto the back of the buggy, next to the instrument panel. Hold until set.

Leave the plastic dome unpainted.

5 Paint the outside of the *base* black and paint the ends of the dowels silver.

6 Next, paint the top half of your buggy with silver paint and let it dry.

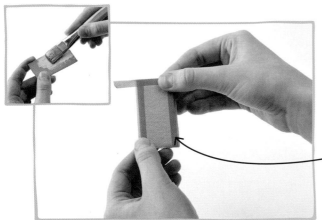

Frame the solar panel with silver washi tape, once the paint has dried.

7 Cut a piece of cardstock 1³/₁₆ in x 2³/₈ in (3 cm x 6 cm). Paint it silver. Fold washi tape around it, glue it to the 4-in (10-cm) dowel, and paint that silver, too.

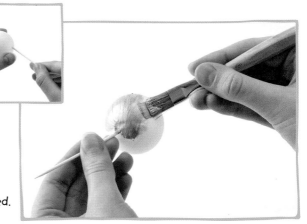

8 For a receiver, insert a toothpick into the other half of the ping-pong ball. Glue it in place and paint the whole thing silver.

If you don't have a silver umbrella, just paint one silver instead.

9 To make a satellite dish, open out the cocktail umbrella and snip off the stick inside it. Glue the 2³/₈-in (6-cm) dowel to the top of the umbrella and paint the dowel silver.

10 Use the grid method to copy the window shapes on page 102. Cut them out and glue in place, then add yellow stickers for headlights.

Add a silver-painted
toothpick antenna.

Radio dish for talking
to spacecraft orbiting
the Moon.

Solar power can drive
a buggy's motors.

Pressurized interior lets
astronauts work without
spacesuits.

High-powered
radio link with
Earth.

11 Add red stickers for taillights and thumb tacks for flashing lights, then glue on the instruments. Roll the buggy backward to wind up the rubber band, let go, and watch it zoom along!

The rubber band is
stretched when the buggy
is pulled backward, then
springs back when released
to drive the buggy forward.

SPACE SCIENCE DRIVING DESIGNS

In the 1970s, NASA's open Lunar Roving Vehicle extended how far astronauts could explore—and the amount of rock samples they could collect—during the Apollo Moon missions. Desert tests on Earth have shown that sealed vehicles could help future astronauts even more. The latest rover designs for both the Moon and Mars all feature sealed compartments for astronauts, with six wheels for added stability.

Apollo Lunar Roving Vehicle

NASA "Small Pressurized Rover"

NASA "Mars Rover Vehicle
Navigator"

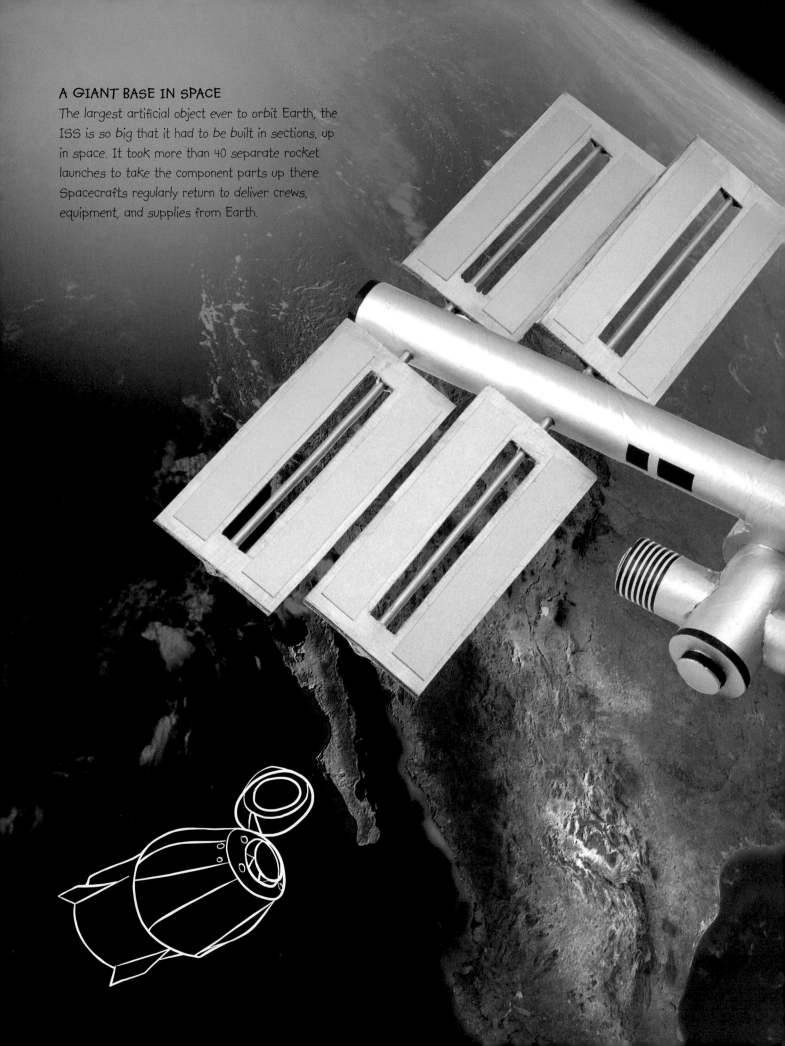

A GIANT BASE IN SPACE

The largest artificial object ever to orbit Earth, the ISS is so big that it had to be built in sections, up in space. It took more than 40 separate rocket launches to take the component parts up there. Spacecrafts regularly return to deliver crews, equipment, and supplies from Earth.

INTERNATIONAL SPACE STATION

The International Space Station (ISS) is an incredible feat of space engineering. It was built by 15 different countries working together over 13 years, but you can make this model version without any help in just a few hours.

The ISS is powered by solar panels that follow the Sun; you can tilt the solar panels on your space station, too.

The space station has a central beam, or "truss structure," to connect all the components and modules.

Painted bottle caps are "docking stations."

The space station can be seen as a bright light moving fast across the night sky. You can follow it online using NASA's ISS tracker.

MAKE YOUR OWN
SPACE STATION

This project is made of interlocking cardboard tubes, with rotating "solar panels" on dowels fitted through the longest tube. Add as many of the decoration ideas as you want.

Time 2 hours, plus drying time	**Difficulty** Hard

WHAT YOU NEED

Silver paint

White glue

Paintbrush

Ruler

Pencil

Scissors

Compass

Masking tape Tape measure

Washi tape

Wide cardboard tube (Tube A) approx. 11¾ in (30 cm) long, 2³⁄₁₆ in (5.5 cm) diameter

Thumb tack

Medium cardboard tube (Tube D) approx. 4 in (10 cm) long, 1⁹⁄₁₆ in (4 cm) diameter

Small cardboard tube (Tube C) approx. 2³⁄₈ in (6 cm) long, 1⁹⁄₁₆ in (4 cm) diameter

Long cardboard tube (Tube B) approx. 23½ in (60 cm) long, 1⁹⁄₁₆ in (4 cm) diameter

4 dowels 18 in (46 cm) long

5 bottle caps

Stiff cardstock

White cardstock

Yellow or gold cardstock

1 Measure the diameter of Tube A and halve it to find the radius. Draw a circle of that radius on cardstock roughly 9⅞ in x 4 in (25 cm x 10 cm).

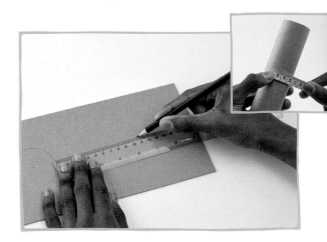

2 Draw a line across the cardstock from the circle. Measure the circumference of Tube B, subtract ¾ in (2 cm), then mark off that distance on the line.

3 With your compass set to the same radius as Step 1, put the point on the line so that the pencil is touching the mark and draw another circle.

4 Then draw a second circle, with a radius ³⁄₈ in (1 cm) larger, around both of the original circles.

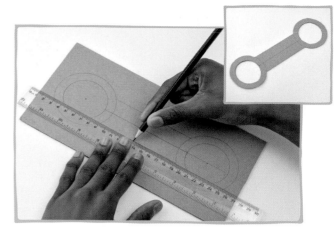

5 Draw two parallel lines, ³⁄₄ in (2 cm) on either side of the center line, for a central strip. Then cut around the outline and the inner circles.

6 Gently bend the central strip of cardstock into a curved shape. This is your connector to hold the central tubes (Tube A and Tube B) together.

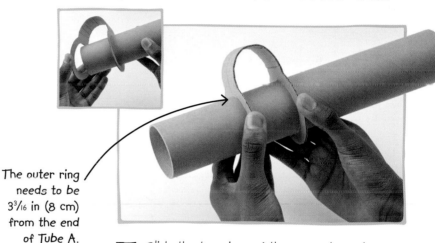

The outer ring needs to be 3³⁄₁₆ in (8 cm) from the end of Tube A.

7 Slide the two rings of the connector onto Tube A and ease them along until there is 3³⁄₁₆ in (8 cm) of tube at one end.

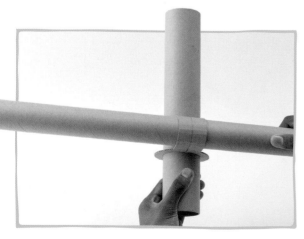

8 Slot Tube B halfway through the curved strip so it sits at a right angle to Tube A. Tube B is the truss structure and Tube A the main module.

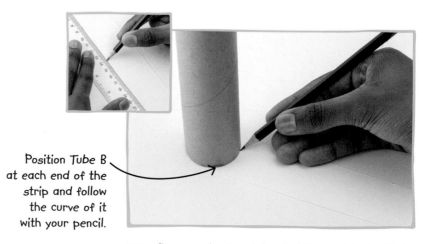

Position Tube B at each end of the strip and follow the curve of it with your pencil.

9 Draw and cut a strip of white cardstock 1⁹⁄₁₆ in x 8⁵⁄₈ in (4 cm x 22 cm). At either end, draw around Tube B. Cut along the lines to shape the ends.

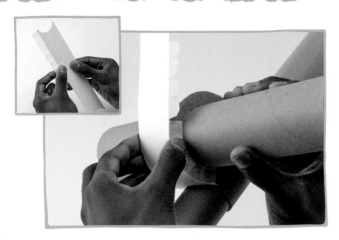

10 Attach small pieces of masking tape along one side of the strip. Position it over the two rings of the connector and stick the strip to one ring.

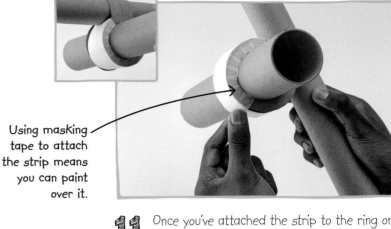

Using masking tape to attach the strip means you can paint over it.

11 Once you've attached the strip to the ring on one side, repeat on the other side to attach it to the other ring.

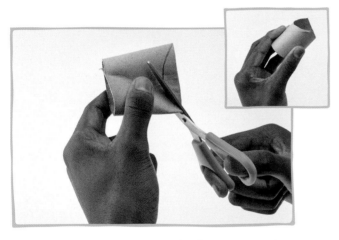

12 For another ISS module, flatten one end of Tube C and draw a curve across it. Cut out the curve, then mold the tube back into shape.

13 Position the other, straight end of Tube C on a piece of cardstock. Draw around it and cut out the circle.

14 Apply glue around the edge of the circle, then stick it to the flat end of Tube C to strengthen it. Hold until set.

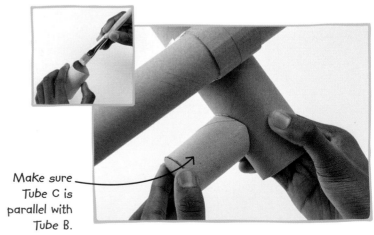

Make sure Tube C is parallel with Tube B.

15 Glue the curved end of Tube C to Tube A, halfway along the 3³/₁₆-in (8-cm) section you left in Step 7.

16 Repeat Steps 12–15 with *Tube D* to make the final ISS module. Attach it to *Tube A* on the opposite side to *Tube C*, in line with it.

The central truss structure of the ISS is about 356 ft (108.5 m) long.

Keep these tubes parallel with Tube B.

Line up *Tubes C* and *D* on either side of *Tube A*.

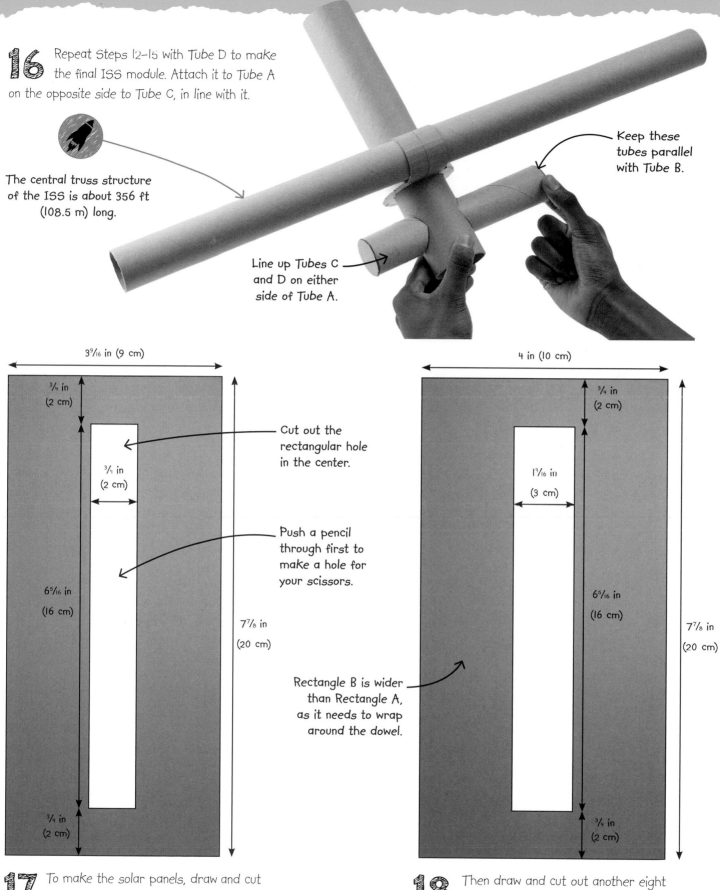

3⁹⁄₁₆ in (9 cm)

¾ in (2 cm)

¾ in (2 cm)

Cut out the rectangular hole in the center.

Push a pencil through first to make a hole for your scissors.

6⁵⁄₁₆ in (16 cm)

7⅞ in (20 cm)

¾ in (2 cm)

Rectangle B is wider than Rectangle A, as it needs to wrap around the dowel.

4 in (10 cm)

¾ in (2 cm)

1³⁄₁₆ in (3 cm)

6⁵⁄₁₆ in (16 cm)

7⅞ in (20 cm)

¾ in (2 cm)

17 To make the solar panels, draw and cut out eight rectangles of cardstock to the measurements above (Rectangle A).

18 Then draw and cut out another eight rectangles of cardstock to the slightly wider measurements above (Rectangle B).

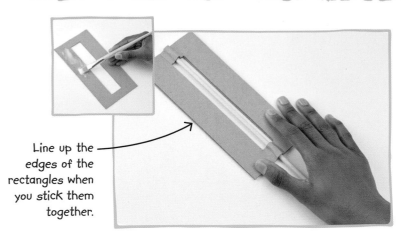

Line up the edges of the rectangles when you stick them together.

19 To assemble the solar panels, apply glue to either end of four Rectangle As. Stick one end of a dowel onto each one and allow to set.

20 Glue a Rectangle B onto each of the four Rectangle As, bending each one around the dowel to sandwich it between the cardstock.

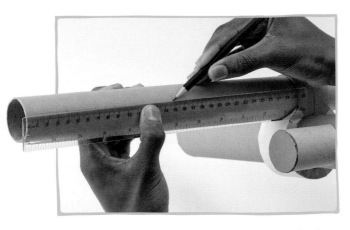

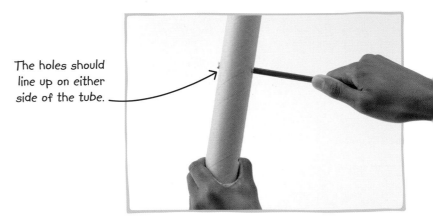

The holes should line up on either side of the tube.

21 Draw a line along one side of Tube B, about halfway up it. Make marks on the line 1⁹/₁₆ in (4 cm) and 5¹⁵/₁₆ in (15 cm) from each end.

22 Repeat Step 21 to mark the same points on the other side of the tube. Push a pencil through to make a hole at each of the eight marks.

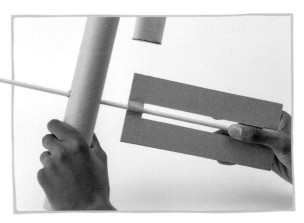

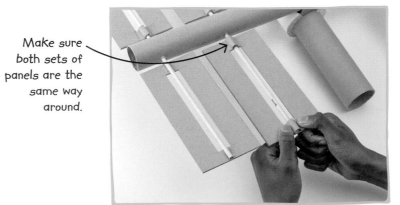

Make sure both sets of panels are the same way around.

23 Carefully push each of the four dowels through the four pairs of holes on either side of Tube B.

24 Repeat Steps 19–20 to make the four remaining solar panels for the other end of each dowel, on the opposite side of Tube B.

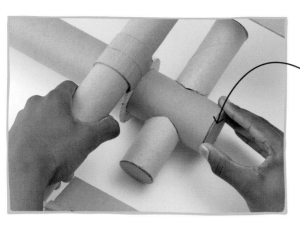

Stick the circle to the end of Tube A nearest Tubes C and D.

25 Make a circle of cardstock the diameter of Tube A (see Step 1) and glue it to the end of that tube. Then make two more circles to glue to either end of Tube B, too.

26 Cut two rectangles of cardstock 9 in x 2⅜ in (23 cm x 6 cm). Glue them together so they're double-thickness, then glue them to the open end of Tube A. Leave all to set.

27 Glue a bottle cap onto the end of each tube to add some "docking stations." Then you're ready to begin painting your space station.

The ISS orbits Earth at an altitude of 205–255 miles (330–410 km).

Rotate the dowels to tilt your solar panels.

The station modules contain sections such as living quarters and laboratories.

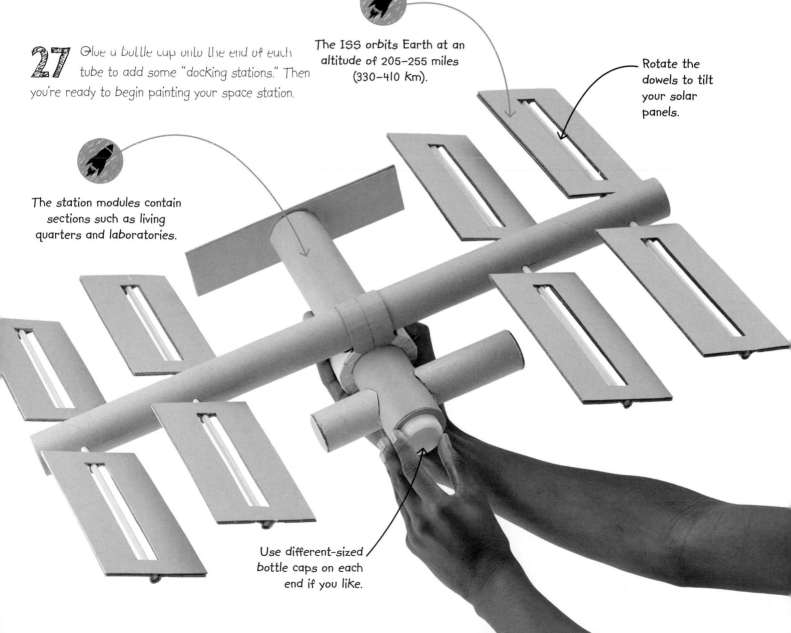

Use different-sized bottle caps on each end if you like.

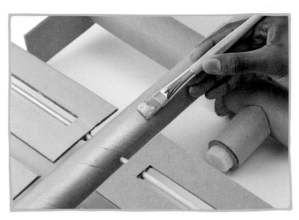

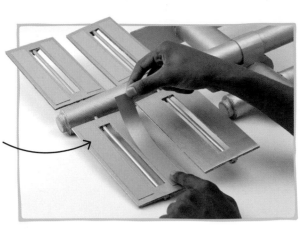

Glue the gold card to the flat side of the solar panels.

28 Paint the whole model silver, giving it a second coat if necessary, to completely cover everything. Leave to dry.

29 Cut 16 strips of gold cardstock 1 in × 7¹/₁₆ in (2.5 cm × 18 cm). Stick two onto each solar panel, on either side of the central hole.

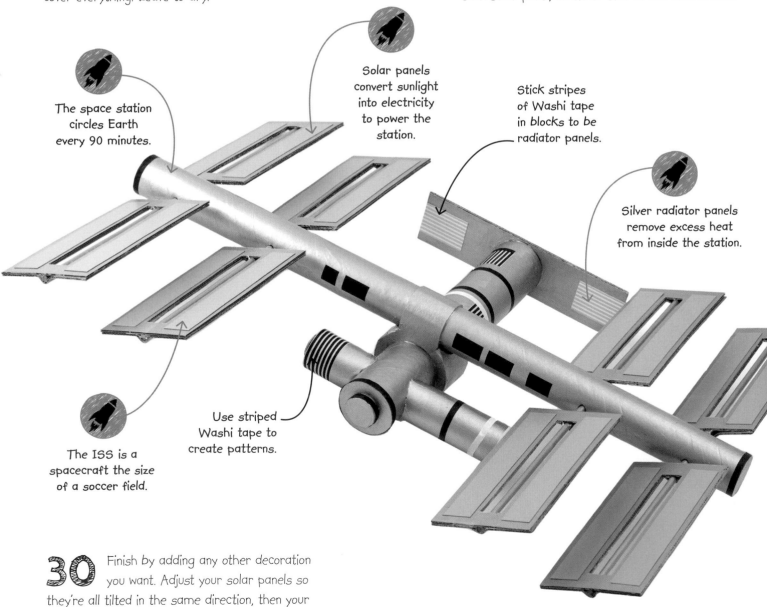

The space station circles Earth every 90 minutes.

Solar panels convert sunlight into electricity to power the station.

Stick stripes of Washi tape in blocks to be radiator panels.

Silver radiator panels remove excess heat from inside the station.

The ISS is a spacecraft the size of a soccer field.

Use striped Washi tape to create patterns.

30 Finish by adding any other decoration you want. Adjust your solar panels so they're all tilted in the same direction, then your space station is ready for astronauts.

SPACE SCIENCE
LIFE ON BOARD

Since 2000, the ISS has hosted more than 260 astronauts, who usually stay for six months or more. The main modules are the laboratories, where the crew study the effects of weightlessness on everything from metals and crystals to plants and small animals. By experimenting on themselves, too, astronauts can learn more about how to keep crews healthy on future missions to Mars and beyond.

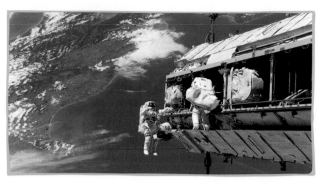

Astronauts do spacewalks to repair and upgrade the ISS and run experiments in the vacuum of space.

Connected by the central truss, the ISS has a series of airtight modules that provide a space bigger than a six-bedroom house.

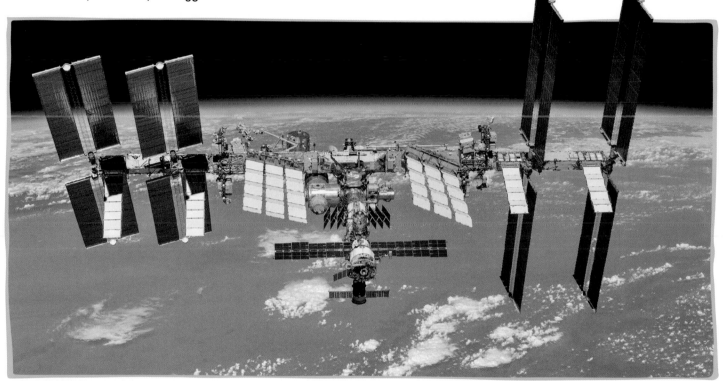

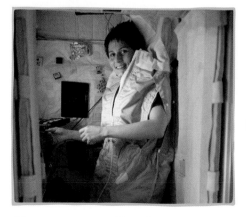

There are seven cabins where astronauts can slide into a sleeping bag to stop themselves floating away as they snooze.

The Cupola module has a large window looking down at Earth and is a favorite place to relax.

Scientists are studying how to grow fresh food in space without sunlight or Earth's gravity.

TARGET APPROACHING
DOCKING EXPERIMENT

Astronauts need excellent coordination skills, and this experiment is a really good test of how well you can judge trajectories, speed, and distance. Can you "dock" the *ball* in the target?

Pull this string to drop the *ball* from the cup.

The string takes the ball directly over the target.

Time the release of the ball at exactly the right moment to get it in the hole.

A pizza box makes a good target, but you could use any broad-topped box.

HIGH-SPEED DOCKING

Spacecrafts arriving at the International Space Station (ISS) need to dock on target after moving at very high speeds. The station itself is already traveling at an average speed of 17,227 miles (27,724 km) per hour on its orbit around Earth.

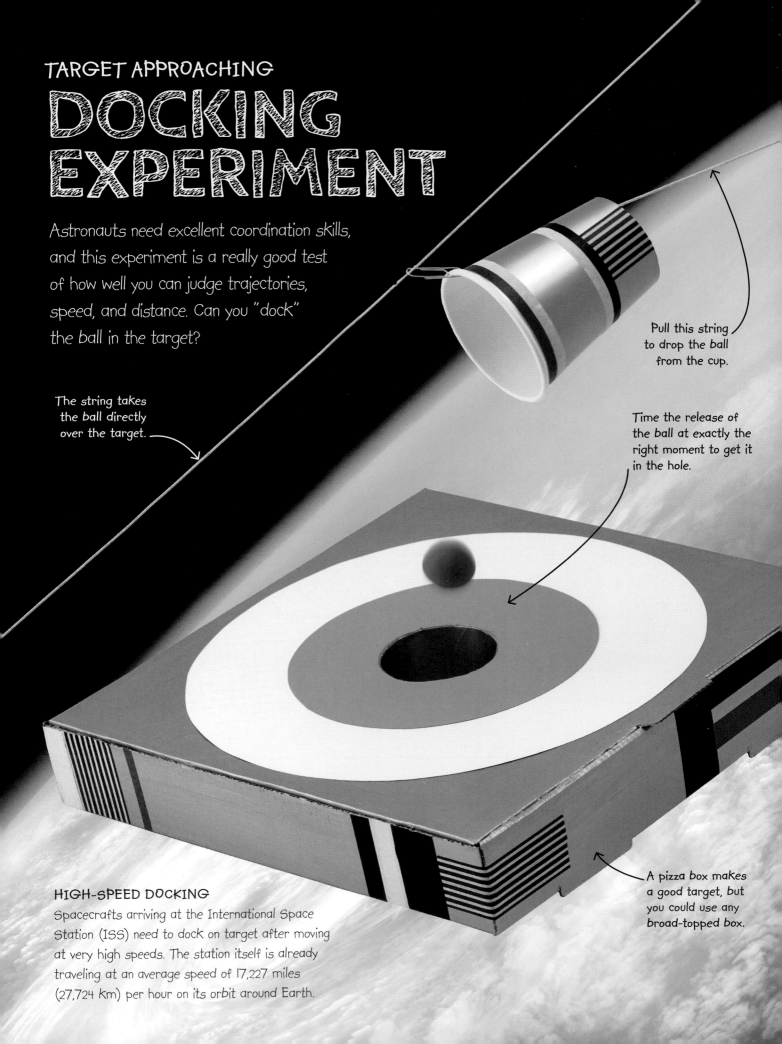

MAKE YOUR OWN
DOCKING STATION

We've used a pizza box for a target. (You can order these online.) Our box and cups are decorated to match other projects in this book, but use whatever you have available—it will still be just as challenging to get the ball in the hole!

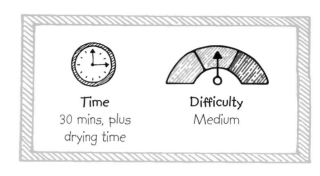

Time
30 mins, plus drying time

Difficulty
Medium

WHAT YOU NEED

Ruler

Scissors

Pencil

White glue

Paintbrush

Thumb tack

Clean pizza box (or any broad-topped box)

White cardstock

Gold paper

Washi tape

Modeling clay ball

6½-ft (2-m) piece of string (approx.)

3-ft (1-m) piece of string (approx.)

2 silver paper cups (or paint them silver yourself)

Small plate

Silver paint

Paper clip

Large plate

2 chairs

1 Fold the pizza box (they usually arrive flat and need assembling), then apply glue to all the flaps on the lid. Push the lid flaps inside the box and press the sides of the box firmly.

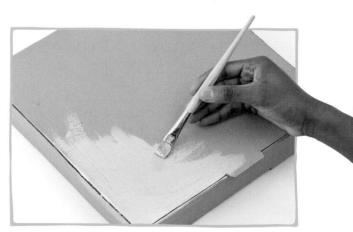

2 Paint the outside of the box silver, giving it a second coat if necessary, to cover the box completely. Leave to dry.

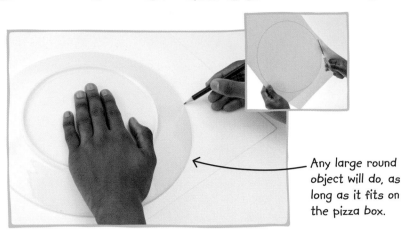

Any large round object will do, as long as it fits on the pizza box.

3 Lay a dinner plate on a large sheet of white cardstock and draw around it with a pencil. Cut out the circle.

4 Repeat Step 3, but with a smaller plate and drawing onto gold paper instead. (If you don't have any, just use white paper and paint it gold.)

Patterns around a dock help the astronaut or computer zero in on the target.

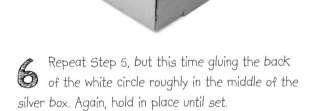

5 Apply glue to the back of the gold circle and stick it approximately in the middle of the white circle. Hold until the glue has set.

6 Repeat Step 5, but this time gluing the back of the white circle roughly in the middle of the silver box. Again, hold in place until set.

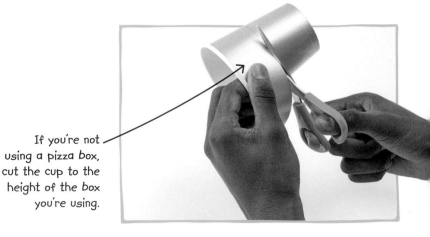

If you're not using a pizza box, cut the cup to the height of the box you're using.

7 Stand your paper cup next to the pizza box. Rotate the cup so you can mark the height of the pizza box on the side of it at regular intervals.

8 Join up the marks with a pencil line, then carefully cut along the line. Your cup is now the same height as the pizza box.

9 Paint the inside of the cup silver. You may need two coats of paint to cover it completely. Leave to dry.

10 Turn the cup upside down and place it approximately in the middle of the gold circle. Draw around it with a pencil.

11 Push a pencil through the central circle to make a hole, then insert your scissors into the hole and cut along the pencil line.

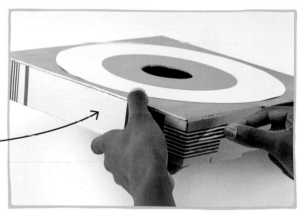

We've decorated our docking station to match the space station (see page 110).

12 If you want, decorate the box with paint or Washi tape. You could match it to the space station or rocket projects in the book.

13 Apply glue to the base of the paper cup, place it in the central hole, and press down on the inside of the base until the glue has set.

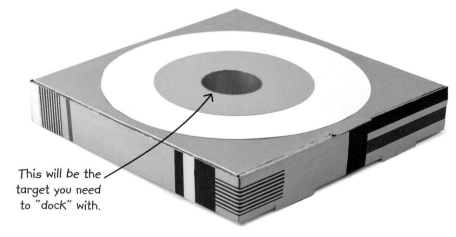

This will be the target you need to "dock" with.

14 Your docking station is now ready, complete with central target. Next, you have to make your "incoming spacecraft."

15 The second paper cup will be your incoming spacecraft. If you want to, decorate it with Washi tape to match the docking station.

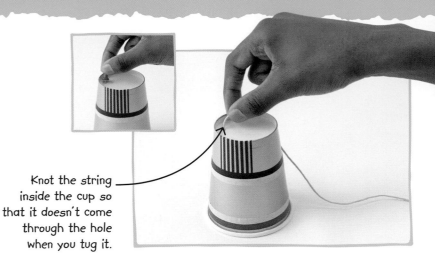

Knot the string inside the cup so that it doesn't come through the hole when you tug it.

16 In the *base* of the cup, near the edge, make a hole with a *thumb* tack. Thread the *shorter* piece of string through the hole and *knot* the end.

17 Make another hole with the thumb tack near the top of the cup, in line with the hole you made for the string.

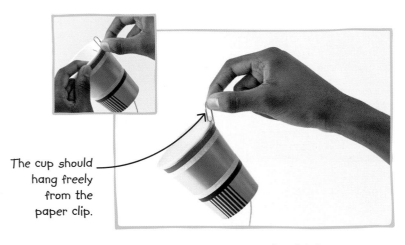

The cup should hang freely from the paper clip.

18 Unbend the paper clip slightly so you can slot the end of it through the hole you've just made, then close the paper clip back up.

19 Thread one end of the longer piece of string through the paper clip.

Tie the long string to each chair so that the string slopes downward.

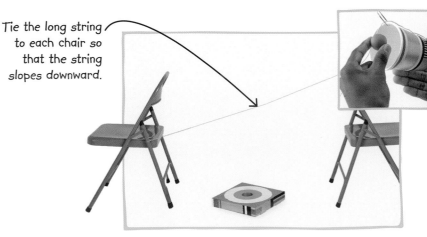

20 Put the docking station on the floor between two chairs. Tie the long string to the chairs. Put the modeling clay ball in the cup, then slide it up to the top of the long string.

21 Holding the short string loosely in one hand, let go of the cup. As it starts sliding down toward the lower chair, pull on the short string to tip up the cup and release the ball so that it lands in the target.

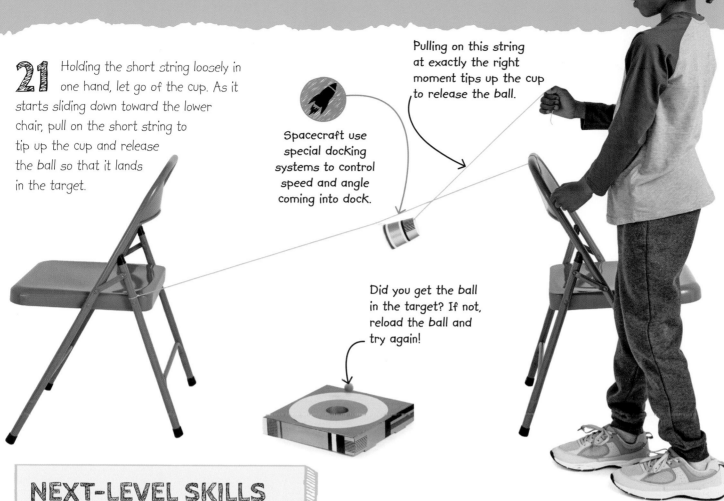

Spacecraft use special docking systems to control speed and angle coming into dock.

Pulling on this string at exactly the right moment tips up the cup to release the ball.

Did you get the ball in the target? If not, reload the ball and try again!

NEXT-LEVEL SKILLS

Want to test your docking skills even further? When spacecrafts arrive to dock on a space station, the station is on its own orbit path. So both spacecrafts are moving on their own trajectories, which makes it even harder to dock safely. Try something similar yourself:
• Place the docking station on a sheet between the chairs, to one side of the string.
• Ask a friend to pull the sheet slowly across the floor, under the string.
• Let the cup slide down the string. Can you release the ball at exactly the right moment to land it in the hole when both the cup and target are moving in different directions?

SPACE SCIENCE
DOCKING CHALLENGES

To line up with a target such as a space station, spacecrafts must change angle and speed by tiny amounts. Large rocket engines are too powerful for this delicate job, so instead small rockets called thrusters are used. The docking system computes the distance to the target and its relative speed before an astronaut or computer uses visual patterns around the target to complete the final approach.

Spacecraft docking systems use locks that clamp in place once a probe hits the target.

GET A GRIP

REMOTE MANIPULATOR

Ever wished you had an extendable arm? These mechanical extensions move when your fingers move, copying your actions with their robot hand. While most robotic arms in space are operated remotely, this one is directly connected to your brain.

You could decorate the arm to match the space helmet or just paint it white or silver.

ROBOT ARMS

Robotic tools let astronauts carry out delicate tasks remotely. On the International Space Station (ISS), there are several external robot arms that help the crew carry out repairs to the outside of the ISS. This cuts down how many times astronauts have to risk going outside the space station.

A simple set of strings connects your own fingers to those of the robot hand.

The hand's fingers work in the same way as your own, curling up when the strings are pulled.

MAKE YOUR OWN
ROBOT ARM

This project uses a grid to transfer and scale up the template while keeping everything in proportion. We've added decoration to match the space helmet (see pages 84–91), but leave it plain if you prefer.

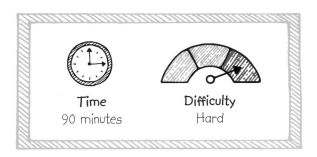

Time
90 minutes

Difficulty
Hard

WHAT YOU NEED

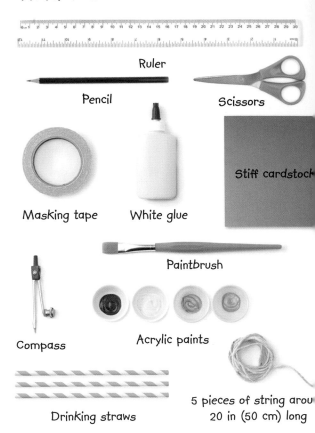

Ruler

Pencil

Scissors

Stiff cardstock

Masking tape   White glue

Paintbrush

Compass

Acrylic paints

Drinking straws

5 pieces of string around 20 in (50 cm) long

TEMPLATES

To copy and enlarge these shapes, use the grid method: draw a grid of squares on your cardstock, then copy the shapes in each square on this template into the squares on your card.

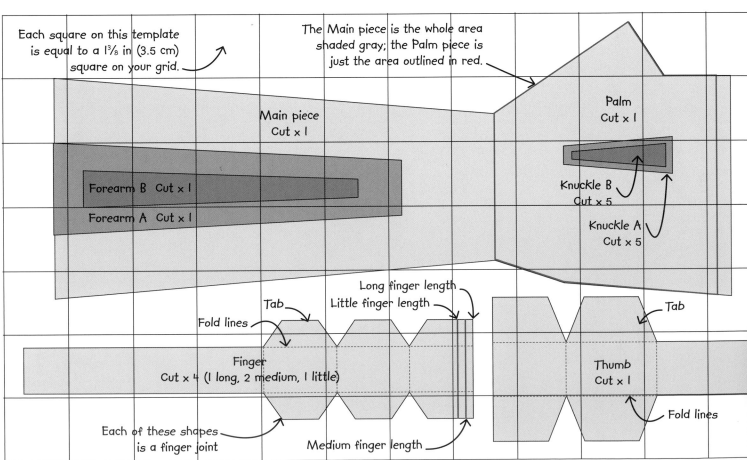

Each square on this template is equal to a 1⅜ in (3.5 cm) square on your grid.

The Main piece is the whole area shaded gray; the Palm piece is just the area outlined in red.

Main piece
Cut x 1

Palm
Cut x 1

Forearm B Cut x 1

Forearm A Cut x 1

Knuckle B
Cut x 5

Knuckle A
Cut x 5

Long finger length
Little finger length

Tab

Fold lines

Tab

Finger
Cut x 4 (1 long, 2 medium, 1 little)

Thumb
Cut x 1

Fold lines

Each of these shapes
is a finger joint

Medium finger length

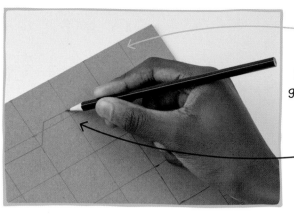

Each square on your grid matches a square on the template.

Copy the shapes as they appear in each square, one square at a time.

1 On a large piece of cardstock, draw a grid of squares 1⅜ in × 1⅜ in (3.5 cm × 3.5 cm). Use the grid to copy the Finger shapes onto the card.

2 Once you have copied each of the four Finger shapes onto the cardstock, cut them out. Paint one side of each piece black and leave to dry.

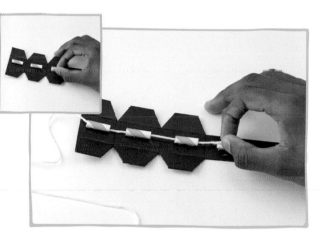

3 Cut 16 pieces of drinking straw ¾ in (2 cm) long. Glue one to the middle of each finger joint. Once the glue has set, thread a piece of string through each row of straws.

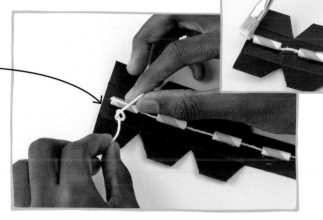

This knot will hold the string in place and stop it from pulling through.

4 At the fingertip ends of each piece of string, tie a knot. Glue the knot in place at the end of the piece of straw.

5 Check the template to see where the fold lines are for the fingers, then crease the tabs of each Finger piece along those lines.

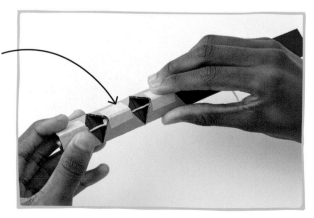

Use masking tape so that you can paint over it later.

6 These are your finger joints. Secure the two tabs of each joint together with a small piece of masking tape.

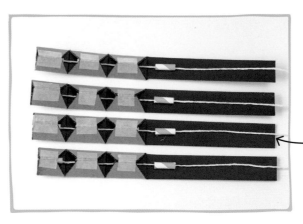

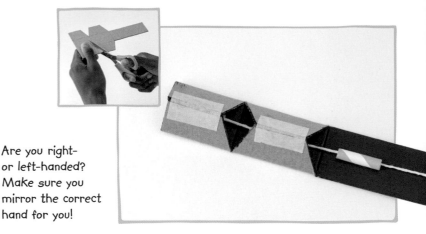

Are you right- or left-handed? Make sure you mirror the correct hand for you!

7 Line up the Finger pieces in the same order as the fingers on your hand: medium, long, medium, little.

8 Repeat Steps 1–6, but this time to make the Thumb piece, and cutting three pieces of drinking straw 1 in (2.5 cm) long instead.

By using a grid, you can copy and enlarge (scale up) a shape and keep it in proportion.

Position the fingers in order on the Main piece.

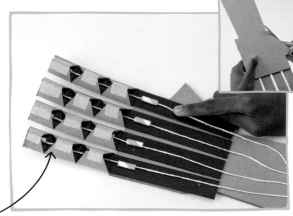

9 Using the grid method again, copy the Main piece template onto card. Cut it out and copy it to make a second piece, then glue them together.

10 Glue the Finger pieces in place on the Main piece. Trim away any bits that stick out where the hand tapers to the wrist.

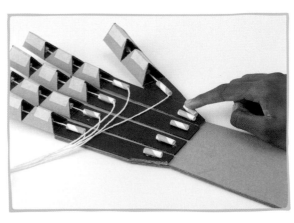

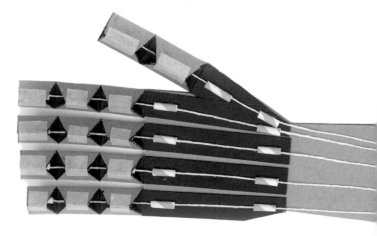

11 Stick the Thumb piece in place, then cut five pieces of drinking straw ¾ in (2 cm) long. Glue them to the ends of the pieces at the wrist.

12 Once the glue has set, thread the loose ends of the strings through the additional pieces of straw, too. Gently pull them taut.

The main robot arm on the ISS can stretch to 58 ft (17.6 m) long.

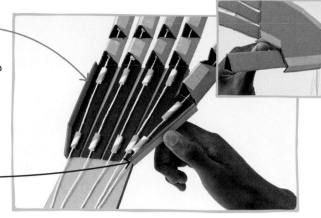

13 Cut two strips of cardstock 5½ in x ⅜ in (14 cm x 1 cm). Tape one strip along the palm edge of the Main piece and trim off any excess.

Save the excess you trim off this strip to use between the finger and thumb.

14 Tape the second strip to the other edge of the Main piece, then tape the offcut from that strip between the thumb and first finger, too.

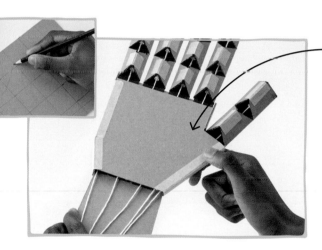

The Palm piece boxes in the strings and straws to protect them.

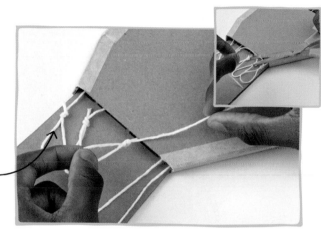

Make each loop large enough to fit your fingers through.

15 Using a grid again, make the Palm piece. Position it over the strings and straws and tape it to the top edges of the three strips.

16 About ¾ in (2 cm) away from the wrist edge of the Palm piece, tie a loop in each piece of string. Trim any excess string.

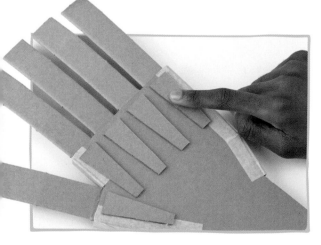

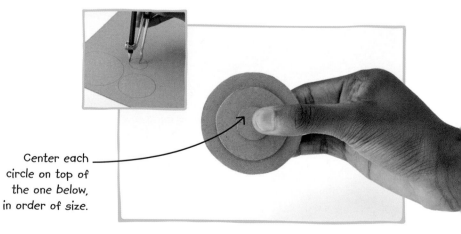

Center each circle on top of the one below, in order of size.

17 Use the grid method to draw five Knuckle A shapes from the template. Cut them out and glue them onto the back of the Main piece.

18 Make three cardstock circles: one with a radius of 1⅜ in (3.5 cm), one 1 in (2.5 cm), and one ⅜ in (1 cm). Glue them in a stack and leave to set.

19 Glue the stack of circles onto the back of the hand, and make a wrist strap by cutting a rectangle of cardstock 3³/₁₆ in x 1³/₁₆ in (8 cm x 3 cm). Glue it onto the wrist, and leave to dry.

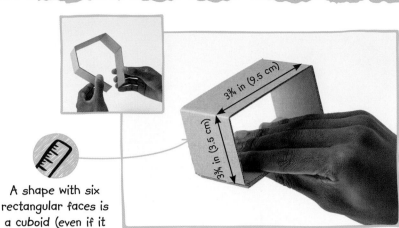

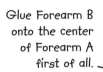

A shape with six rectangular faces is a cuboid (even if it is hollow, with two faces open).

20 Cut two strips of cardstock: one 12³/₄ in x 1⁹/₁₆ in (32.5 cm x 4 cm) and one 15¹/₂ in x 2 in (39.5 cm x 5 cm). Fold and glue the large strip into a cuboid 3³/₄ in x 2³/₁₆ in (9.5 cm x 5.5 cm).

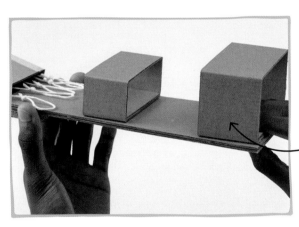

These two cuboids will be your arm straps.

21 Fold and glue the smaller strip into a hollow cuboid 3³/₈ in x 1³/₈ in (8.5 cm x 3.5 cm). Glue both in place on the inside of the Main piece.

Glue Forearm B onto the center of Forearm A first of all.

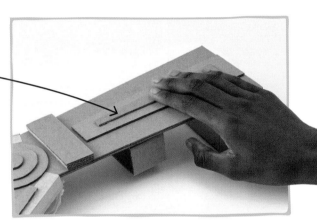

22 Make the Forearm A and Forearm B pieces from the template. Glue B onto A, then glue A onto the back of the Main piece.

23 Paint the fingers, the palm, and the back of the Main piece white. Leave to dry, then add a second coat if needed.

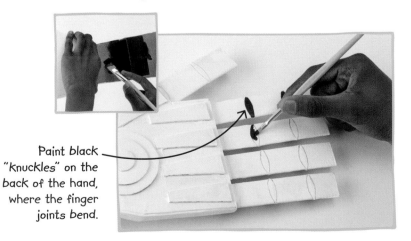

Paint black "Knuckles" on the back of the hand, where the finger joints bend.

24 Paint the inside of the Main piece black, including the arm straps. Paint black "Knuckles," too, then leave all to dry.

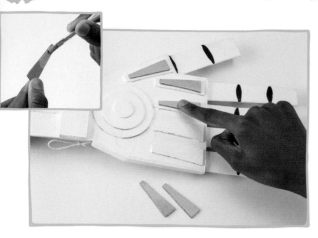

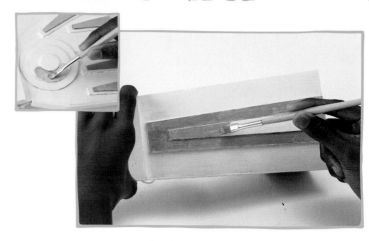

25 Make five Knuckle B pieces and paint them gold. Once dry, glue them onto the Knuckle As, as shown, and leave to set.

26 Apply silver paint to the middle circle and Forearm A. Once dry, paint the top circle and Forearm B with gold paint and leave to dry.

Robot arms in space are linked to controls inside a spacecraft.

These decorations to match the helmet are optional (see page 84).

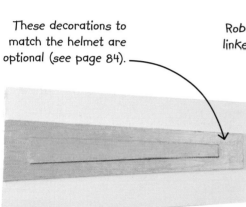

Future robot arms will be able to relay "touch" data to their astronaut operators.

27 Cut a cardstock rectangle 9/16 in x 3 3/16 in (1.5 cm x 8 cm) and paint it gold. Once dry, glue it onto the wrist strap. Leave to dry.

Loop the thumb and forefinger string both over your forefinger.

The ISS "Canadarm" can carry weights equivalent to eight school buses.

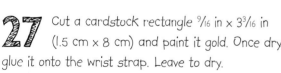

28 Now put those robot fingers to work. Slide your hand through the arm straps and insert your fingers into the loops. As you move your fingers, your robot hand will do the same.

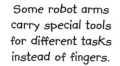

Some robot arms carry special tools for different tasks instead of fingers.

When you wiggle your little finger, your robot finger will move, too.

LANDING CRAFT

Much of what we know about our Solar System comes from probes and rovers that have landed on other planets and moons. So what's the best way to land a vehicle safely on another world? How can you be sure it stays upright and isn't damaged by the impact of the landing? Make these different landers, then run an experiment to find out which one works best.

HAPPY LANDINGS

A successful landing is one where the spacecraft touches down close to upright and is undamaged by the shock of the impact. Making the impact area wide (i.e., spreading out the legs of the vehicle) and using flexible materials to absorb the shock can help achieve this.

Instead of an astronaut, you'll put a ping-pong ball inside your lander to test the impact force.

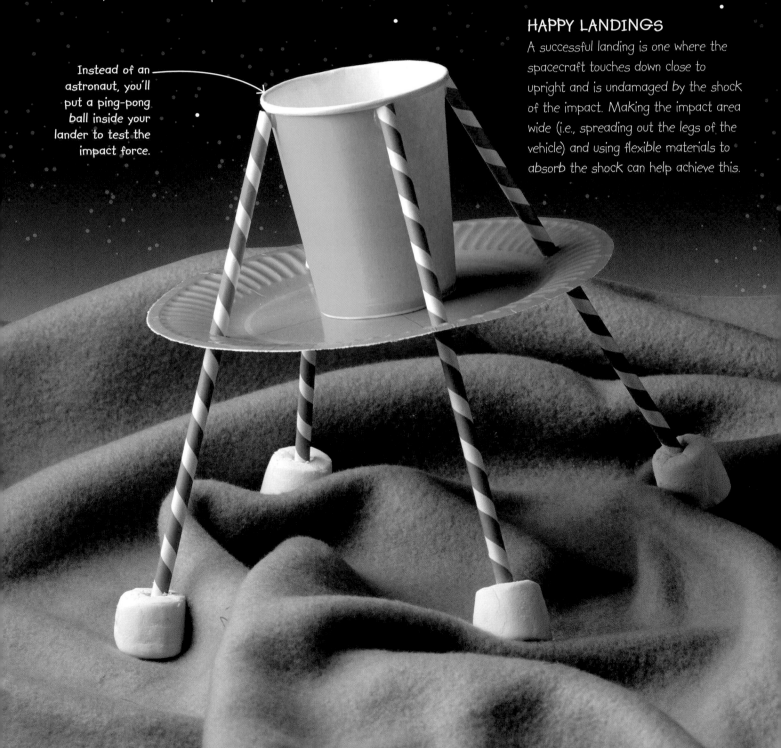

of shock absorber.

The sudden change of speed on landing can create a shock that may damage a spacecraft.

Use a rumpled blanket to create an uneven Moon terrain as an extra test of your lander's stability.

Experiment to compare how stable the different "leg" options are.

MAKE YOUR OWN
MOON LANDER

We've used different colors for each lander, but you can use whatever you have. The key thing is the variety of leg designs to test stability and the different types of shock absorbers to test how they handle the impact of landing.

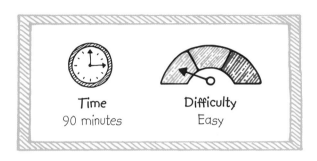

Time
90 minutes

Difficulty
Easy

WHAT YOU NEED

Ruler

Pencil

3 paper fasteners

Paintbrush

Ping-pong ball

Stiff cardstock

White cardstock

Scissors

Protractor

Colored paper cups

Colored paper plates

Modeling clay

White glue

Masking tape

Extra-long ruler

4 marshmallows

4 paper drinking straws

Notebook

3 rubber bands

Tin can

MAKE THE YELLOW LANDER

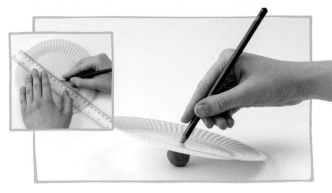

1 Measure the plate's widest point to find the center. With modeling clay behind it for safety, use a pencil to push a small hole in the plate's center.

2 Next, measure to find the center of the cup's base, too. Use your pencil to make a small hole in the center of the cup's base.

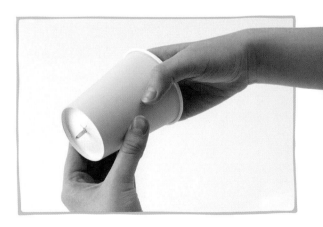

3 Push the pointed end of a paper fastener down through the hole in the base of the paper cup.

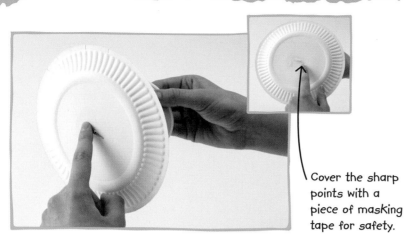

Cover the sharp points with a piece of masking tape for safety.

4 Push the plate onto the paper fastener and open out the points so the paper fastener sits flat against the plate, then cover with tape.

5 To make the "legs" of your lander, draw four rectangles 3³⁄₁₆ in × 5⁵⁄₁₆ in (8 cm × 13.5 cm) on a piece of cardstock. Cut them out.

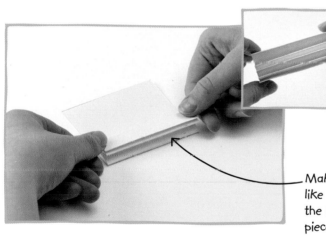

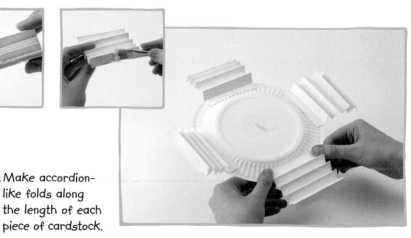

Make accordion-like folds along the length of each piece of cardstock.

6 Starting along a short edge of one leg, make a series of folds. Fold in alternate directions every ⁵⁄₈ in (1.5 cm) or so. Repeat for all four legs.

7 Apply glue along the end fold of each leg, then stick them to the underside of the plate, spacing them evenly around the circumference.

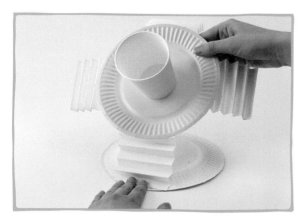

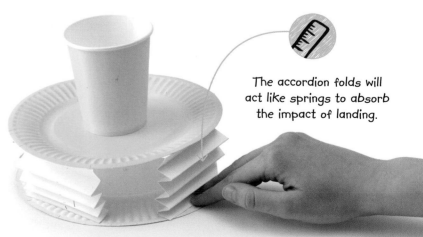

The accordion folds will act like springs to absorb the impact of landing.

8 Position another paper plate below the lander, face-down. Glue the other end of one leg to the second paper plate.

9 Repeat for the other three legs, again spacing them evenly around the circumference of the second plate.

MAKE THE BLUE LANDER

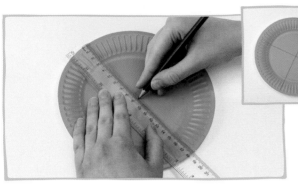

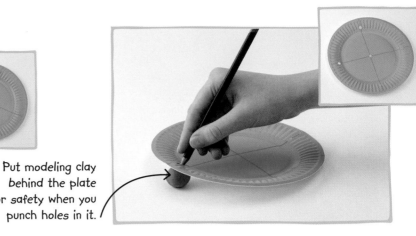

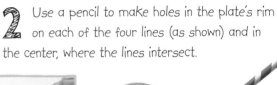

Put modeling clay behind the plate for safety when you punch holes in it.

1 Draw a line through the center of the paper plate, then using a protractor to measure the angle, draw a second line at 90° to the first one.

2 Use a pencil to make holes in the plate's rim on each of the four lines (as shown) and in the center, where the lines intersect.

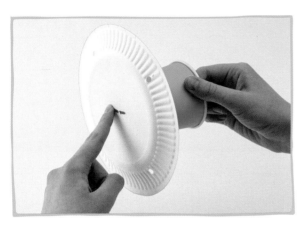

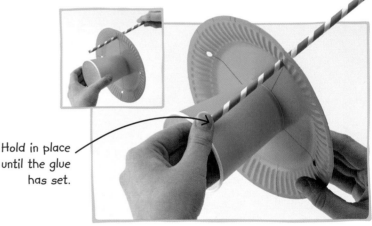

Hold in place until the glue has set.

3 Make a hole in the center of the cup's base. Push a paper fastener through it and through the central hole of the plate. Open it out and tape over the sharp ends, as before.

4 Push a straw through each of the holes in the plate's rim, then glue one end of each straw to the cup, just below the top.

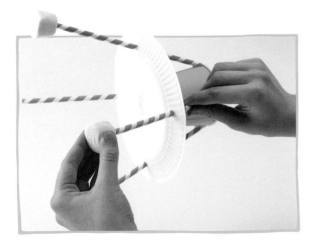

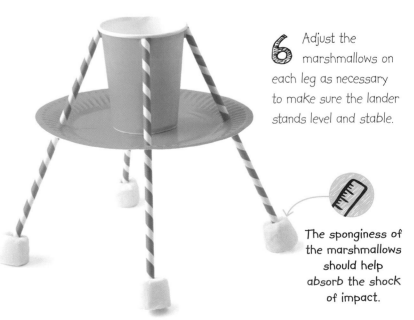

6 Adjust the marshmallows on each leg as necessary to make sure the lander stands level and stable.

The sponginess of the marshmallows should help absorb the shock of impact.

5 Push a marshmallow gently onto the other end of each straw to complete the legs of this lander.

MAKE THE RED LANDER

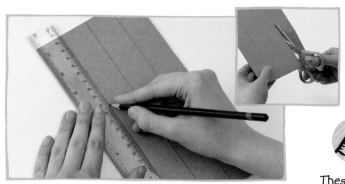

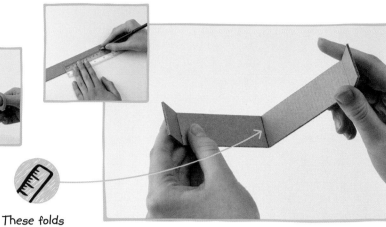

1 Cut a rectangle of cardstock 9 in x 4¾ in (23 cm x 12 cm). Divide the cardstock up into four long strips 1³/₁₆ in (3 cm) wide. Cut out the strips.

These folds should act as shock absorbers on impact.

2 Along each strip, mark off points at 1 in (2.5 cm), then 4⅛ in (10.5 cm), then 8⅛ in (20.5 cm). Bend the cardstock at those points.

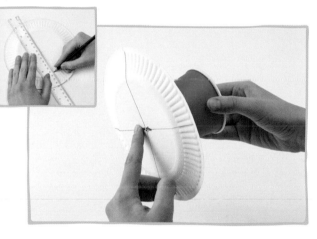

Make sure the shorter fold is nearest the plate.

3 On the plate's underside, draw two lines through the center at right angles. (Use a protractor to measure 90°.) Attach the cup and plate with a paper fastener and tape over the sharp ends.

4 Using the ends with the shorter fold, glue each strip over one of the four pencil lines on the plate's underside. Hold until set.

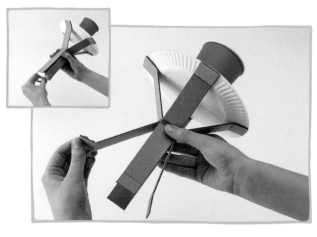

5 Carefully slide the rubber band over the end of the four strips. Move it along to sit at the 4⅛-in (10.5-cm) fold line.

6 Open out the folds again below the rubber band and stand the lander level on the final fold.

Landers have multiple legs to spread their weight in case they land on a crumbly surface.

DO THE EXPERIMENT

Height	Yellow lander	Blue lander	Red lander
12 in (30 cm)			
16 in (40 cm)			
20 in (50 cm)			
24 in (60 cm)			

1 Prepare a chart for the results of your experiment. Make a column for each lander and rows for the different heights you are going to drop it from.

2 Put a ping-pong ball "astronaut" in the cup of the lander you're going to try first.

Landing craft range from delicate robot rovers to Moon landers carrying astronauts.

Will the lander keep the ping-pong ball in the cup, or will it get bounced out by the impact?

Shock absorbers reduce the impact on delicate parts of a lander, such as the electronics or a human crew.

Use the ruler to make sure each lander falls from the same height.

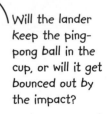

Which lander will have the best shock absorbers?

Will the landers stay level when they hit the ground, or will they fall over?

3 Attach the extra-long ruler to a tin can with two rubber bands and stand beside it. Drop the lander from each of the heights on your chart in succession and record your observations.

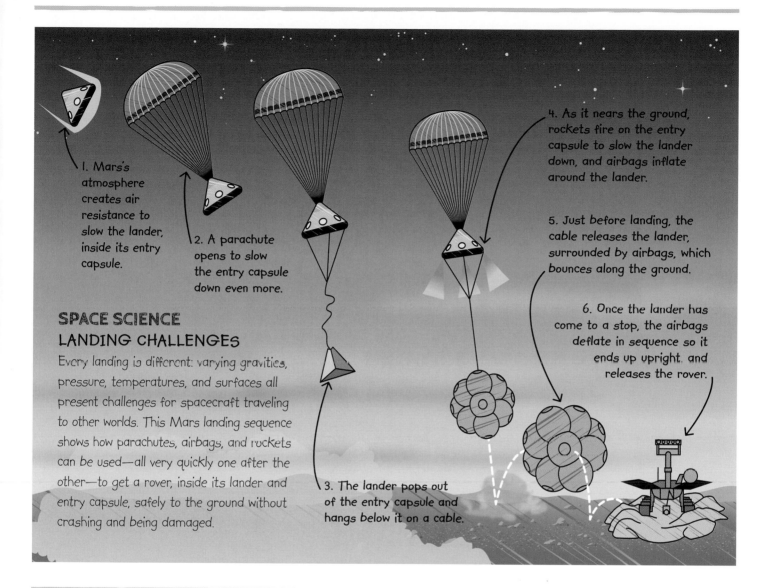

1. Mars's atmosphere creates air resistance to slow the lander, inside its entry capsule.

2. A parachute opens to slow the entry capsule down even more.

SPACE SCIENCE
LANDING CHALLENGES

Every landing is different: varying gravities, pressure, temperatures, and surfaces all present challenges for spacecraft traveling to other worlds. This Mars landing sequence shows how parachutes, airbags, and rockets can be used—all very quickly one after the other—to get a rover, inside its lander and entry capsule, safely to the ground without crashing and being damaged.

3. The lander pops out of the entry capsule and hangs below it on a cable.

4. As it nears the ground, rockets fire on the entry capsule to slow the lander down, and airbags inflate around the lander.

5. Just before landing, the cable releases the lander, surrounded by airbags, which bounces along the ground.

6. Once the lander has come to a stop, the airbags deflate in sequence so it ends up upright, and releases the rover.

TAKE IT FURTHER

Once you've tested your different designs to see how upright they land and how well the shock absorber options work, you could add more variables, such as:
• use a heavier ball instead of a ping-pong ball;
• drop the landers on an uneven surface to see if they still land upright;
• make variations with three or five legs, to see how that affects their ability to stay upright. Don't forget to record your observations in your notebook for each variable.

STARFINDING

Do you want to be able to read the night sky? This chapter is all about developing your astronomy skills. Learn how to spot the features of the Moon and how to find stars and recognize the constellations, wherever you are on Earth. Follow our useful tips on preparation and planning and you'll be rewarded by sightings of stars, space stations, planets, meteor showers, and maybe even a comet! With this introduction to starfinding, you'll soon be able to unlock the secrets of the universe.

HOW TO SEE THE STARS

Do you want to be able to read the night sky? As you head out to discover more about the universe for yourself, follow the simple steps for success outlined here. This preparation and equipment will help you stay safe and comfortable and make the most of your stargazing sessions.

SPOTTING STARS

On a dark night, you might see around 3,000 stars once your eyes have adjusted to the darkness. If you have binoculars or a telescope, you can see even more details.

PREPARE AHEAD
STARGAZING

The only essential equipment is warm clothing, as you'll be standing or sitting still. Optional extras include: a waterproof sheet to sit on and keep equipment dry if the ground is wet; binoculars; a flashlight, ideally red (see right); a pen, notebook, and clock to record the times of sightings; and a compass and book, chart, or starfinding app to help you navigate the night sky.

WHAT YOU NEED

Warm clothing

Waterproof sheet (optional)

Binoculars (optional)

Notepad (optional)

Pen (optional)

Clock or watch (optional)

Flashlight (preferably red)

Star chart (called a planisphere) or astronomy book (optional)

Compass (optional)

Smartphone or tablet with starfinding apps (optional)

MAKING A RED FLASHLIGHT

Red light doesn't interfere with your night vision, so a red flashlight is useful for starfinding. To make one, cover the light of your flashlight with a clear red plastic film and hold it in place with elastic bands.

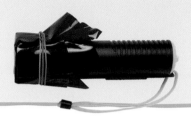

TIPS FOR SUCCESS

• **Light pollution:** Try to get away from the glow of artificial light and find an open space if you can to get a clearer view of the sky.

• **Weather:** Check to make sure it will be a clear night, as clouds will block your view of the stars. Clear nights can be cold, though, so dress warmly.

• **The Moon:** Avoid stargazing when there's a full or nearly full Moon, as it gives off too much light. Choose a night around a new Moon instead.

• **Adjust your eyes:** Once outside, let your eyes adjust to the darkness for 20 minutes so you can see the faintest stars much more clearly. Use a red flashlight to keep your night vision once you have it.

• **Binoculars:** With binoculars or a telescope, you can see farther and enhance the detail of stars. Hold your hands very steady or rest them on a stable surface.

STAYING SAFE

Never head off starfinding alone. Always go with an adult. If you start to feel slightly cold, go back inside to warm up—don't wait until you're already chilly.

WHAT CAN YOU SEE?
THE NIGHT SKY

Most of the objects you can see in the night sky are stars—blazing balls of gas like our own Sun but much farther away. They vary hugely in size, brightness, color, and distance, but astronomers often imagine that they are sitting on a vast celestial sphere wrapped around the Earth.

THE MILKY WAY

All the stars you can spot when you look up at the sky lie within our home galaxy, the Milky Way (see pages 60–61). Seen from outside, the Milky Way looks like a flat spiral with a central bulge of stars, but because we're inside the spiral, we see a band of light that wraps around the sky and is brightest toward the center. This milky-white band gave the "Milky Way" its name.

STAR MOVEMENT

The sky changes through the course of each night, so you can see different constellations as Earth rotates. The stars also seem to drift westward from one night to the next. A compass and star chart or app can help you work out where to look to find constellations or planets.

SPACE SCIENCE
THE CELESTIAL SPHERE

To map all the hundreds of thousands of stars, galaxies, and other objects in the sky, astronomers imagine that they are all fixed points on a huge hollow rotating ball, with Earth spinning inside it. This "celestial sphere" seems to rotate around "celestial poles" above Earth's North and South Poles. Astronomers divide the sky into 88 separate areas called constellations, which fit together like a jigsaw puzzle to cover the entire sphere (see pages 148–149).

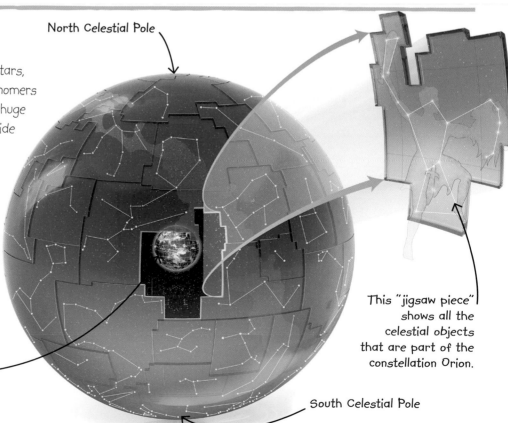

North Celestial Pole

This "jigsaw piece" shows all the celestial objects that are part of the constellation Orion.

Where you are on Earth determines which bit of the celestial sphere you can see.

South Celestial Pole

STAR PATTERNS
CONSTELLATIONS

Astronomers use constellations, imaginary areas that fit together to form the celestial sphere (see page 147), as a way to help them find stars and other objects. To navigate the night sky and know where and when to look for an object in space, learn how to find the distinguishing stars and shapes of the constellations—such as the three stars of Orion's Belt.

Betelgeuse, at Orion's right shoulder, has a diameter hundreds of times bigger than that of the Sun.

The three stars of Orion's Belt are (from east to west) Alnitak, Alnilam, and Mintaka. Alnilam is much farther away from Earth than Alnitak and Mintaka.

Rigel, at Orion's left heel, is the brightest star in the constellation. It gives off many tens of thousands of times more light than the Sun.

ORION IN THE SKY
One of the sky's most famous constellations, Orion lies on the celestial equator (midway between the two celestial poles), so it can be easily seen from both Earth's Northern and Southern Hemispheres.

MAPPING THE NIGHT SKY

As shown in this example of Orion, ancient stargazers imagined patterns in the night sky to be creatures, objects, or gods. Later astronomers developed those ideas into the celestial sphere used today.

1 Long ago, people imagined patterns in the stars and named them after figures and objects.

2 They called the large patterns constellations, and also gave names to some smaller patterns, called asterisms.

3 In 1928, constellations were redefined to include not just the stars but all space objects in the surrounding area, too.

SPACE SCIENCE
STAR DISTANCES

Although Orion's stars sit together on the celestial sphere as we look at them, they're actually at very different distances from Earth.

ORION'S STARS
- Betelgeuse - 500 light-years
- Bellatrix - 250 light-years
- Rigel - 860 light-years
- Alnitak - 1,250 light-years
- Mintaka - 1,200 light-years

The actual placement of the stars in relation to each other in space.

The segment of celestial sphere that shows Orion.

Earth

0   100   200   300   400   500   600   700   800   900   1,000   1,100   1,200   1,300

Time for star's light to reach Earth (in years)

KEEP YOUR EYES OPEN ...
WHAT ELSE IS UP THERE?

While distant stars remain the same from night to night and year to year, many nearby objects move through the sky at different speeds. These include the International Space Station (see pages 110–119), planets, meteors, and even comets. Look for them when you're out starfinding.

COMETS

Comets are huge balls of ice and dust; when they get near the Sun, their icy surface evaporates to release a trail of gas and dust that looks like a glowing tail. Most really bright comets take centuries or even longer to orbit the Sun, but astronomers are good at spotting them—keep an eye on newspapers and astronomy websites or apps to find out when a new bright comet is approaching and how to see it.

METEORS

You can spot meteors on most nights. When tiny rocks and dust particles from space fall into Earth's atmosphere at high speed, they heat up to create a meteor (or shooting star) as they burn away. At certain times, when Earth passes through dust left behind by a comet, meteors appear in showers that seem to come from a particular constellation. The chart below shows when and where you can spot them.

YEARLY METEOR SHOWERS

NAME	PEAK DATE	SOURCE CONSTELLATION
Quadrantids	January 3–4	Boötes
Lyrids	April 22–23	Lyra
Eta Aquariids	May 6	Aquarius
Delta Aquariids	July 30	Aquarius
Perseids	August 12–13	Perseus
Orionids	October 21–22	Orion
Leonids	October 17–18	Leo
Geminids	December 14–15	Gemini

PLANETS

At night, you can *see* planets with the naked eye. Unlike stars, they don't twinkle because they're much closer to Earth, so they shine steadily and brightly. Some are easier to spot than others: Venus, for example, is the brightest object in the night sky after the Moon, while Mars is the second-brightest and looks a bit reddish. (The picture on the right shows Mars near the Moon during a lunar eclipse.) Just before sunset or just after sunrise is a good time to see some, such as Venus and Mercury. To see the two farthest planets of our Solar System, Uranus and Neptune, you'd need a telescope.

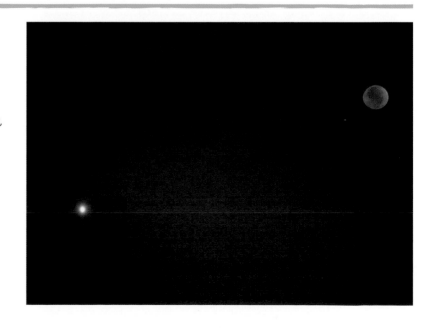

LUNAR LANDSCAPE
THE MOON

The Moon is our nearest neighbor in space, and even with the naked eye there's lots to spot, such as light and dark areas on its surface. Explore it during any phase of the Moon except Full Moon; the sideways light of the other phases casts shadows that help you make out details.

MAPPING THE MOON

On the Moon, you can see a mix of dark areas called seas and lighter, cratered regions called highlands. But if you have binoculars or a telescope, you can also pick out the details of its craters and mountains.

The lunar highlands are the original ancient crust of the Moon.

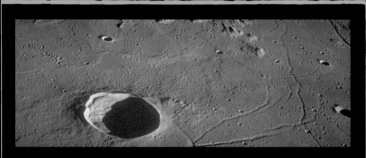

THE MOON'S CRATERS

Craters on the Moon were mostly formed when it was hit by rocks from space early in its history. Later, lava from volcanoes filled the deepest craters to create the dark lunar seas.

The Luna 9 landing site, where in 1966 the first controlled landing was made by a Soviet robot spacecraft.

SPACE SCIENCE
WHAT IS A LUNAR ECLIPSE?

At Full Moon, we see the Moon fully lit by the Sun's rays. Sometimes, however, the Sun, Earth, and Moon line up so that the Moon passes through Earth's shadow in an event called a lunar eclipse. The Full Moon goes dark for several hours and may even appear red sometimes.

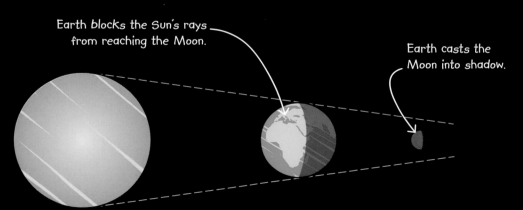

Earth blocks the Sun's rays from reaching the Moon.

Earth casts the Moon into shadow.

The Sun   Earth   The Moon

The Sea of Tranquility is a huge crater that was flooded by lava 3.5 billion years ago.

The Sea of Crises is a small but distinctive round sea.

The US Apollo 11 landing site, where in 1969 people first stood on the Moon.

Lunar seas are made of a dark volcanic rock called basalt.

THE NIGHT SKY IN THE NORTH
THE NORTHERN HEMISPHERE

Astronomers divide the celestial sphere into two hemispheres (half spheres), each centered on a celestial pole (one of the two fixed points in the sky that don't move as Earth spins on its axis). Stargazers at locations north of Earth's equator can see all the stars in the sky's Northern Hemisphere at one time or another, as well as many from the Southern Hemisphere (see pages 156–157).

NORTHERN SKY

Most Northern Hemisphere constellations were named by astronomers from the ancient Middle East and Greece.

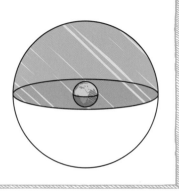

FINDING THE NORTH CELESTIAL POLE

To find the pole, follow these steps to locate a bright star called the Pole Star or Polaris, which sits almost at the North Celestial Pole.

1 Use a compass to find north. The celestial pole sits above Earth's North Pole, so the Pole Star is always due north in the sky.

2 Spot the "saucepan" pattern of the Big Dipper (also known as the Plough). Find the two stars on the east side of it and draw an imaginary line between them.

3 Extend that imaginary line about five times farther through the sky and it will take you north. The Pole Star will be the next bright star you come across.

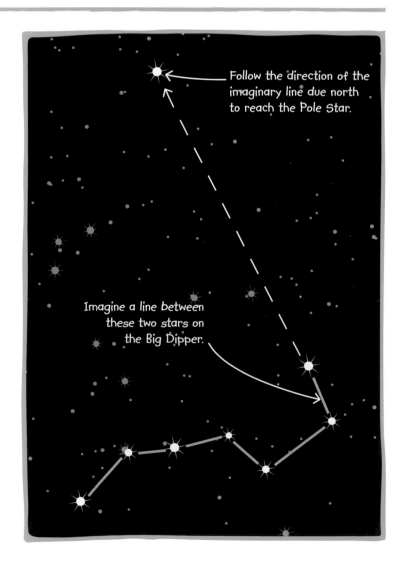

Follow the direction of the imaginary line due north to reach the Pole Star.

Imagine a line between these two stars on the Big Dipper.

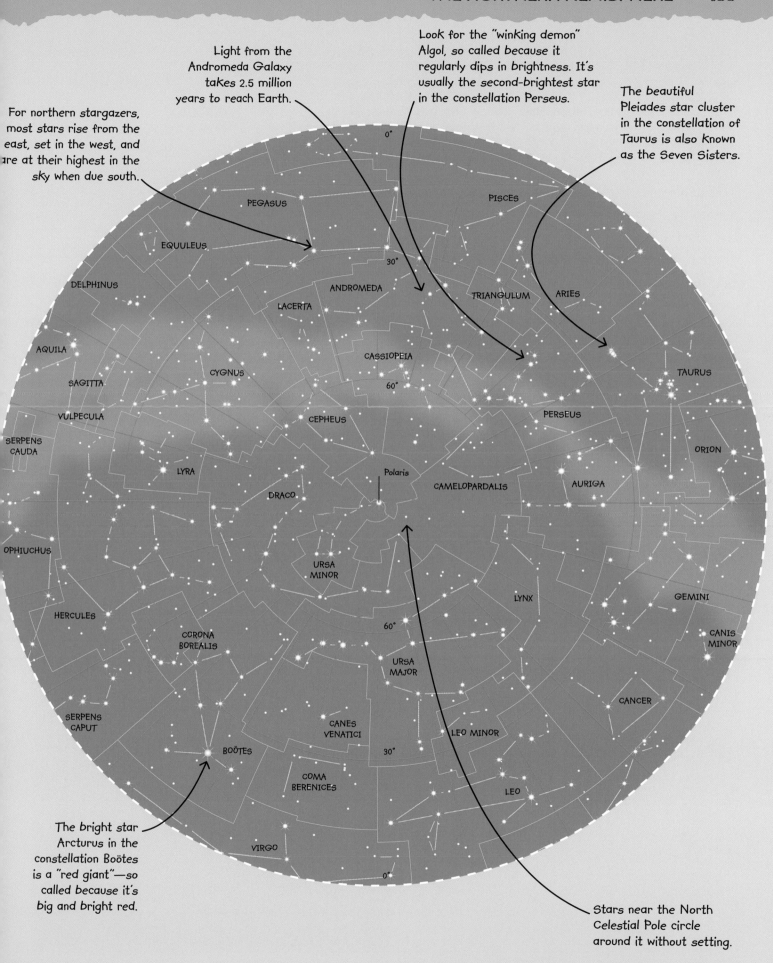

Light from the Andromeda Galaxy takes 2.5 million years to reach Earth.

Look for the "winking demon" Algol, so called because it regularly dips in brightness. It's usually the second-brightest star in the constellation Perseus.

The beautiful Pleiades star cluster in the constellation of Taurus is also known as the Seven Sisters.

For northern stargazers, most stars rise from the east, set in the west, and are at their highest in the sky when due south.

The bright star Arcturus in the constellation Boötes is a "red giant"—so called because it's big and bright red.

Stars near the North Celestial Pole circle around it without setting.

0°
30°
60°
Polaris
60°
30°
0°

PEGASUS
EQUULEUS
DELPHINUS
AQUILA
SAGITTA
VULPECULA
SERPENS CAUDA
LYRA
OPHIUCHUS
HERCULES
CORONA BOREALIS
SERPENS CAPUT
BOÖTES
VIRGO
COMA BERENICES
CANES VENATICI
URSA MAJOR
URSA MINOR
DRACO
CEPHEUS
CYGNUS
LACERTA
ANDROMEDA
CASSIOPEIA
PISCES
TRIANGULUM
ARIES
PERSEUS
TAURUS
ORION
CAMELOPARDALIS
AURIGA
GEMINI
CANIS MINOR
LYNX
CANCER
LEO MINOR
LEO

THE NIGHT SKY IN THE SOUTH
THE SOUTHERN HEMISPHERE

The southern half of the celestial sphere rotates around the South Celestial Pole. There's no convenient bright star to mark this spot in the sky, but there are plenty more things to see. Stargazers at locations south of Earth's equator can see all the stars in the sky's Southern Hemisphere at one time or another, as well as many of those from the Northern Hemisphere (see pages 154–155).

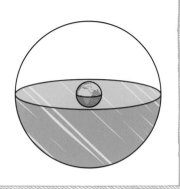

SOUTHERN SKY

European astronomers from the 15th–18th centuries named many official constellations of the Southern Hemisphere.

FINDING THE SOUTH CELESTIAL POLE

This pole doesn't have a single star to mark its position, but you can find the spot using imaginary lines from brighter stars.

1 First, use a compass to find south. The celestial pole sits above Earth's South Pole.

2 Find the constellation of Crux, the Southern Cross: four very bright stars, forming a cross. Imagine a line extending south from the longer arm.

3 Look east from Crux to find the Southern Pointers: two bright stars in the constellation Centaurus. Imagine a line between them, and another line at right angles to that, midway along it.

4 Extend this line until it crosses the line running south from Crux. Where they intersect marks the South Celestial Pole.

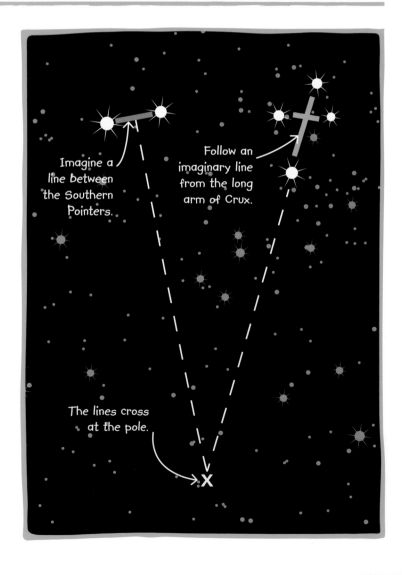

Imagine a line between the Southern Pointers.

Follow an imaginary line from the long arm of Crux.

The lines cross at the pole.

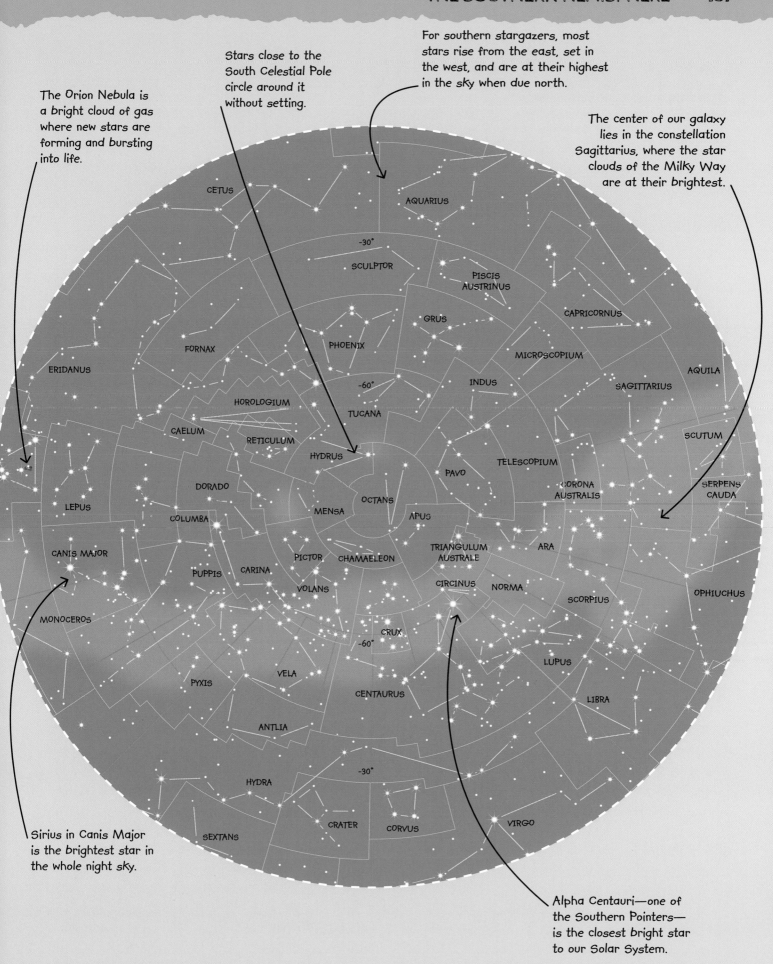

The Orion Nebula is a bright cloud of gas where new stars are forming and bursting into life.

Stars close to the South Celestial Pole circle around it without setting.

For southern stargazers, most stars rise from the east, set in the west, and are at their highest in the sky when due north.

The center of our galaxy lies in the constellation Sagittarius, where the star clouds of the Milky Way are at their brightest.

Sirius in Canis Major is the brightest star in the whole night sky.

Alpha Centauri—one of the Southern Pointers— is the closest bright star to our Solar System.

CETUS

AQUARIUS

-30°

SCULPTOR

PISCIS AUSTRINUS

GRUS

CAPRICORNUS

PHOENIX

FORNAX

MICROSCOPIUM

AQUILA

ERIDANUS

-60°

INDUS

SAGITTARIUS

HOROLOGIUM

TUCANA

SCUTUM

CAELUM

RETICULUM

HYDRUS

TELESCOPIUM

PAVO

SERPENS CAUDA

DORADO

OCTANS

CORONA AUSTRALIS

LEPUS

MENSA

APUS

ARA

COLUMBA

CHAMAELEON

TRIANGULUM AUSTRALE

CANIS MAJOR

PICTOR

CIRCINUS

NORMA

OPHIUCHUS

PUPPIS

CARINA

VOLANS

SCORPIUS

MONOCEROS

CRUX

LUPUS

-60°

VELA

PYXIS

CENTAURUS

LIBRA

ANTLIA

-30°

HYDRA

SEXTANS

CRATER

CORVUS

VIRGO

GLOSSARY

ACCELERATION
An increase in the speed of an object.

AIR RESISTANCE
A force (also known as drag) that slows down objects as they move through air.

ANTENNA
A rod- or dish-shaped device that can transmit and receive radio signals.

ASTERISM
A small group of stars with a distinctive shape, useful for finding your way around the sky.

ASTEROID
A small, roughly shaped chunk of rock or metal orbiting the Sun.

ASTEROID BELT
A donut-shaped region of the Solar System, between the orbits of Mars and Jupiter, where most asteroids orbit.

ASTRONAUT
A person trained to travel and live in space. Russian ones are called cosmonauts, and Chinese ones are called taikonauts.

ASTRONOMY
The scientific study of space and all the objects in it.

ATMOSPHERE
A layer of gas around a planet.

BOOSTER
A small rocket attached to a larger one to give extra power during launch.

CELESTIAL
Relating to the sky or outer space. An object outside Earth's atmosphere is a celestial body.

CELESTIAL SPHERE
An imaginary sphere around Earth, used by astronomers to measure positions in the sky.

COMET
A space object made mostly of ice and dust. When a comet approaches the Sun, its ice warms up and vaporizes, creating a glowing head and tail.

CONSTELLATION
One of 88 divisions of the celestial sphere that fit together like a puzzle to map the night sky.

CORE
The hot center of a planet or star.

COSMONAUT
A Russian astronaut.

CRATER
A bowl-shaped dent in the surface of a planet, moon, asteroid, or comet.

CRUST
A thin, solid outer layer of a planet or moon.

DENSITY
The amount of matter in a certain amount of space. A denser object has greater mass than a less dense one of the same size.

DOCK
Where a spacecraft joins with another spacecraft or space station in space.

ECLIPSE
When an object passes into the shadow of another object or temporarily blocks it from sight. In a solar eclipse, the shadow of the Moon falls on Earth; during a lunar eclipse, Earth's shadow falls on the Moon.

EQUATOR
An imaginary line around the center of a planet, midway between its two poles.

GALAXY
A collection of stars, gas, and dust held together by gravity.

GRAVITY
A force that attracts things toward heavy objects like planets and stars. On Earth, gravity pulls things toward the ground. In space, it holds moons in orbit around planets, and planets in orbit around stars.

HEMISPHERE
One half of a sphere. Earth is divided into Northern and Southern Hemispheres by its equator.

LATITUDE
A measure of your position north or south of the equator; the equator is 0°, the North Pole has latitude +90°, and the South Pole -90°.

LAUNCH VEHICLE
A rocket-powered vehicle used to send objects into space (such as spacecrafts or satellites).

LIGHT-YEAR
The distance light travels across space in one Earth year.

LUNAR
Relating to the Moon.

MANTLE
A thick, rocky layer between the core and the crust of a planet or moon.

MASS
A measure of how much matter an object contains. Gravity pulls objects with mass toward each other so that they experience a force known as weight.

MATTER
Any material that occupies space and has mass. Matter can take several forms, including solids, liquids, and gases.

METEOR

A blaze of light created when a meteoroid enters Earth's atmosphere, heats up, and burns; also known as a shooting star.

METEOR SHOWER

A series of meteors from the same part of the sky.

METEORITE

A meteoroid that lands on a planet or moon's surface.

METEOROID

A particle of rock, metal, or ice in its own orbit around the Sun.

MILKY WAY

The barred spiral galaxy that contains our Solar System; visible from Earth as a band of faint light across the night sky.

MODULE

Part of a spacecraft with a special function.

MOON

An object made of rock or rock and ice that orbits a planet or asteroid; when capitalized, refers to the Moon that orbits Earth.

NEBULA

A cloud of gas and dust in space, including those where stars are born.

ORBIT

The path an object takes around another when influenced by its gravity.

PARTICLE

An extremely small part of matter.

PHASE

The fraction of the Moon that is lit up by the Sun, as seen from Earth.

PHOTOSPHERE

The Sun's visible surface.

PLANET

A large, spherical object that orbits a star.

POLES

Points at the top and bottom of a space object that stay still as it rotates.

PRESSURIZED

A container that is sealed and filled with air, allowing humans to breathe in space.

PROBE

An uncrewed spacecraft that visits objects in space and sends information back to Earth.

PROPELLANT

A chemical that burns with another one to produce hot gas and provide thrust to a rocket.

RADIATION

Rays of energy, including light and many other types that we cannot see.

ROVER

A vehicle that drives on the surface of a planet or moon.

SATELLITE

A natural or human-made object orbiting another one. Moons are natural satellites.

SOLAR

Relating to the Sun.

SOLAR FLARE

A huge eruption of energy in the Sun's atmosphere.

SOLAR SYSTEM

The Sun and everything that orbits it.

SPACE STATION

A large orbiting spacecraft where a crew can live for weeks or months and carry out research.

SPACESUIT

Sealed, protective clothing worn by an astronaut to protect them in the vacuum of space.

SPACEWALK

A trip outside a spacecraft, made by astronauts in spacesuits in order to repair or install equipment.

STAR

A huge, glowing ball of gas that shines by creating energy in its core.

STELLAR

Relating to stars.

SUN

The star nearest to Earth.

SUNSPOTS

Dark areas sometimes seen on the Sun's surface.

TAIKONAUT

A Chinese astronaut.

TELESCOPE

An instrument that makes distant and faint objects appear closer and brighter.

THRUST

The force from an engine that pushes a rocket or spacecraft forward.

UNIVERSE

All of space and everything in it.

VACUUM

A space with nothing in it, not even air.

VISOR

The windowlike part of a helmet that the wearer can see through.

INDEX

ACKNOWLEDGMENTS

Smithsonian Enterprises:
Kealy Gordon, Product Development Manager
Paige Towler, Editorial Lead
Avery Naughton, Licensing Coordinator
Jill Corcoran, Director, Licensed Publishing
Brigid Ferraro, Vice President, Business Development and Licensing
Carol LeBlanc, President
Reviewer for the Smithsonian:
Mike Hulslander, Manager of Onsite Learning,
National Air and Space Museum, Smithsonian

The publisher would like to thank the following:
Helen Peters for indexing; Jackie Phillips for proofreading; Millie Hughes, Principe Bernardo, Elijah Dixon, and Adrianna Morelos for modeling; Tanya Mehrotra for additional jacket design; Simon Mumford for Illustrator work; Steve Crozier for photo-retouching.

The publisher would like to thank the following for their kind permission to reproduce their photographs:
(Key: a-above; b-below/bottom; c-center; f-far; l-left; r-right; t-top)

8 Alamy Stock Photo: agefotostock / Oleg Rodionov. **23 Alamy Stock Photo:** Susan E. Degginger (b). **24 Alamy Stock Photo:** Nadia Yong. **29 Alamy Stock Photo:** StockStudio (br). **30-31 Alamy Stock Photo:** Valentin Valkov. **37 Dorling Kindersley:** Gary Ombler / Whipple Museum of History of Science, Cambridge (br). **38 Alamy Stock Photo:** Khanisorn Chalermchan; Zoonar GmbH / Michal Bednarek (b). **42 Dreamstime. com:** KarakedT4; Pixelgnome (bc). **43 Dreamstime.com:** Stocksolutions (bl). **45 Dreamstime.com:** Stocksolutions (tl). **57 Dorling Kindersley:** Satellite Imagemap / Planetary Visions (br). **60 ESA:** Hubble & NASA (t, bl); Hubble & NASA, P. Cote (br). **61 ESA:** Hubble & NASA, J. Lee and the PHANGS-HST Team (tl); NASA and The Hubble Heritage Team (STScI / AURA) (cf); Hubble & NASA, J. Barrington (bl). **64-65 Alamy Stock Photo:** Rui Santos. **73 Dorling Kindersley:** Jason Harding / NASA (b).

74-75 Alamy Stock Photo: Stocktrek Images, Inc. **74 123RF.com:** leonello calvetti (b). **84-85 Alamy Stock Photo:** Buradaki. **85 NASA:** (br). **91 ESA:** NASA (br). **100-101 Alamy Stock Photo:** dotted zebra. **109 NASA:** (cb); Regan Geeseman (crb); Kim Shiflett (br). **110-111 Alamy Stock Photo:** Science Photo Library. **119 NASA:** (tr, bl, bc); Roscosmos (c); Cory Huston (br). **120 Alamy Stock Photo:** James Thew (br). **125 NASA:** (br). **126 NASA:** (bc). **136 Dreamstime.com:** Stocksolutions (bl). **140 Dreamstime. com:** Stocksolutions (tl). **144 Shutterstock.com:** vchal. **145 Dreamstime. com:** Stocksolutions (cf); Terracestudio (cla). **146 Alamy Stock Photo:** Imagebroker / Arco / W. Rolfes (b). **146-147 Getty Images:** Tom Grubbe (t). **148 Alamy Stock Photo:** Erkki Makkonen (b). **150 Dreamstime. com:** Solarseven (b). **151 Alamy Stock Photo:** Imaginechina Limited (br); Stocktrek Images, Inc. / Jeff Dai (t). **152 NASA:** (cla). **152-153 123RF.com:** Boris Stromar / astrobobo.

All other images © Dorling Kindersley

DK WHAT WILL YOU MAKE NEXT?

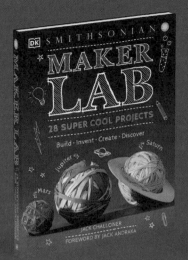

DK SMITHSONIAN
MAKER LAB
28 SUPER COOL PROJECTS
Build · Invent · Create · Discover

JACK CHALLONER
FOREWORD BY JACK ANDRAKA

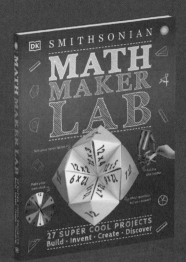

DK SMITHSONIAN
MATH MAKER LAB
27 SUPER COOL PROJECTS
Build · Invent · Create · Discover

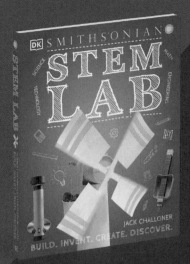

DK SMITHSONIAN
STEM LAB
BUILD. INVENT. CREATE. DISCOVER.

JACK CHALLONER

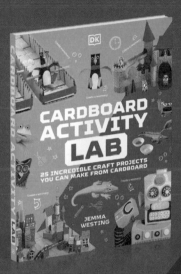

DK
CARDBOARD ACTIVITY LAB
25 INCREDIBLE CRAFT PROJECTS YOU CAN MAKE FROM CARDBOARD

JEMMA WESTING

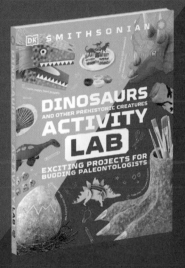

DK SMITHSONIAN
DINOSAURS
AND OTHER PREHISTORIC CREATURES
ACTIVITY LAB
EXCITING PROJECTS FOR BUDDING PALEONTOLOGISTS

DK SMITHSONIAN
GREAT STEM PROJECTS
TRIED-AND-TRUE EXPERIMENTS FOR ALL BUDDING SCIENTISTS

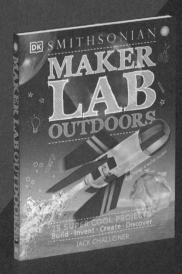

DK SMITHSONIAN
MAKER LAB OUTDOORS
25 SUPER COOL PROJECTS
Build · Invent · Create · Discover
JACK CHALLONER

DK SMITHSONIAN
TECH LAB
AWESOME BUILDS FOR SMART MAKERS

JACK CHALLONER

DK SMITHSONIAN
SPACE ACTIVITY LAB
EXCITING SPACE PROJECTS FOR BUDDING ASTRONOMERS

DK For the curious